The Bathroom Sports Quiz Book

By John Murphy

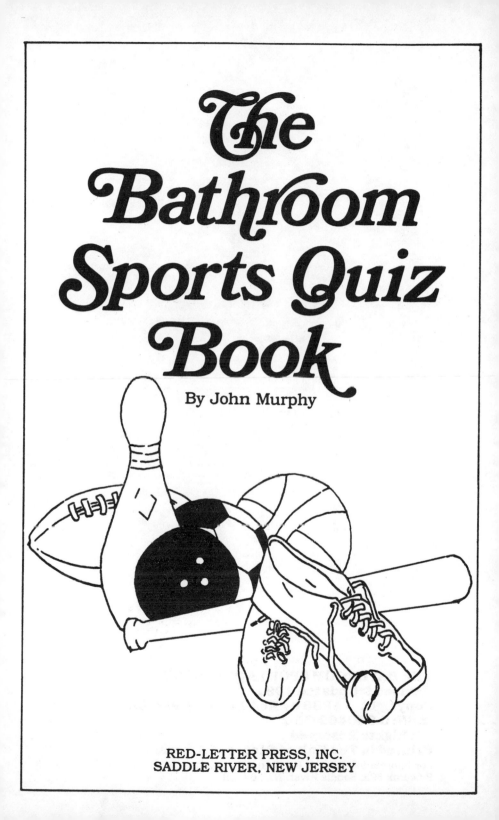

RED-LETTER PRESS, INC.
SADDLE RIVER, NEW JERSEY

THE BATHROOM SPORTS QUIZ BOOK
Revised & Updated 1991
Copyright © 1986 by Red-Letter Press, Inc.
ISBN: 0-940462-05-2
All Rights Reserved
Printed in The United States of America

For information address Red-Letter Press, Inc.,
P.O. Box 393, Saddle River, N.J. 07458

Introduction

We at Red-Letter Press are flushed with enthusiasm to bring you *The Bathroom Sports Quiz Book.*

There's no hot and cold here. Author John Murphy has compiled good, solid stuff—challenging quizzes interspersed with bathroom bafflers throughout the book.

After taking each of the quizzes, you can use The Bathroom Scale on the next page to find out if your sports knowledge is worthy of the throne or in need of some plumbing.

Grateful appreciation is in order to those who've worked on this project - Cyndi Bellerose, Glenn Fraller, Jack Kreismer, Sr., Sylvia Martin and Geoff Scowcroft.

In the end, we must thank John Murphy in particular for this book. It is he, after all, who has brought the sports fan a ticket to the best seat in the house.

Jack Kreismer,
Publisher

The Bathroom Scale

Grade yourself on each of the Sports Quizzes:

Score	Rating
0-2	Throw in the towel
3-4	Down the drain
5-6	Close shave
7-8	Razor-sharp
9-10	Royal flush!

The Bathroom Sports Quiz Book

**BOWL GAMES
FOR THE
SPORTS BUFF**

The Bathroom Library ™

1. What pitcher who retired in 1975 won 25 or more games during a season three times and yet never won the Cy Young Award?

2. Of the current NHL teams, which are the six oldest?

3. What do the initials "O.J." stand for in O.J. Simpson?

4. What are the four Olympic throwing events?

5. Which current NFL team plays its home games in two stadiums each year?

6. Who was the only New Orleans player to lead the NBA in scoring?

7. Of all the big leaguers whose last names begin with the letter C, who has hit the most home runs? Hint: He was born in Puerto Rico.

8. The shortest rebounding champion in NBA history is still playing. Can you think of him?

9. Who scored the winning touchdown in the Baltimore Colts' overtime victory over the New York Giants in the 1958 Championship Game?

10. Only two players won batting championships in seasons in which they struck out more than 100 times. Both played for the Pirates. Name one of them.

Answers

1. *Juan Marichal.*

2. *New York Rangers, Boston Bruins, Chicago Black Hawks, Detroit Red Wings, Montreal Canadians, and Toronto Maple Leafs.*

3. *Orenthal James.*

4. *Javelin, discus, shotput, and hammer.*

5. *The Green Bay Packers. They play in Green Bay and Milwaukee.*

6. *Pete Maravich, in 1977.*

7. *Orlando Cepeda, with 379. (Norm Cash hit 377 homers.)*

8. *6 foot-6 inch Charles Barkley.*

9. *Alan Ameche.*

10. *Roberto Clemente, in 1967, and Dave Parker, in 1977.*

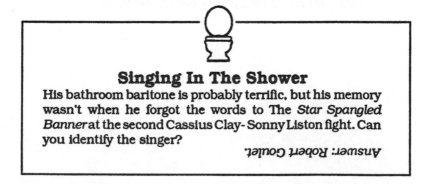

Singing In The Shower

His bathroom baritone is probably terrific, but his memory wasn't when he forgot the words to The *Star Spangled Banner* at the second Cassius Clay- Sonny Liston fight. Can you identify the singer?

Answer: Robert Goulet.

1. In 1950, there were sixteen Major League baseball teams. Eleven of them were located in five cities. Name these five cities.

2. What brother-and-sister team won the Mixed Doubles Championship at Wimbledon in 1980?

3. Who's the only Cy Young Award winner to capture the Award in each league?

4. Who has appeared on the cover of *Sports Illustrated* the most?

5. Name the two teams that played in the first World Series in 1903. Which team won? What two teams played in the World Series in 1904?

6. Only one Knick has ever led the NBA in scoring. Who is this regal player?

7. Two pairs of brothers have pitched no-hitters. Can you get one pair?

8. The only man ever to win the 1500 meter run in consecutive Olympics did it in 1980 and 1984. Name this Briton.

9. Who was the first female to appear on the cover of a Wheaties box?

10. In 1947, 1958 and 1959, N.L. first basemen won Rookie of the Year Awards. Can you think of two of them?

1.   Boston: *Braves* and *Red Sox*; Chicago: *Cubs* and *White Sox*; St. Louis: *Browns* and *Cardinals*; Philadelphia: *Phillies* and *Athletics*; New York: *Giants, Yankees,* and *(Brooklyn) Dodgers.*

2.   John and Tracy Austin.

3.   Gaylord Perry, who did it with Cleveland in 1972 and San Diego in 1978.

4.   Muhammad Ali.

5.   The A. L. Boston Pilgrims defeated the N. L. Pittsburgh Pirates, 5 games to 3, in the first World Series in 1903. There was no World Series in 1904; John McGraw's Giants refused to play the Pilgrims.

6.   Bernard King, in 1985.

7.   Bob Forsch of the Cardinals pitched no-hitters in 1978 and 1983; his brother Ken pitched one for the Astros in 1979. Pascual Perez of the Expos threw a 5-inning no-hitter in 1988; two years later, his brother Melido pitched a 6-inning no-hitter for the White Sox.

8.   Sebastian Coe.

9.   Mary Lou Retton.

10.   Jackie Robinson, 1947; Orlando Cepeda, 1958; and Willie McCovey, 1959. (In Robinson's first year, he played first base while Eddie Stanky played second. The following year Stanky was traded and Robinson was moved to second where he played most of his career.)

1. Isaac Murphy was pleased about his association with the trio of Buchanan, Riley, and Kingman. Why?

2. The man who scored the most points in an NFL game (40 points) also gave up two of Ruth's 60 home runs in 1927. Name him.

3. What are the standard dimensions of a basketball court?

4. Uniform numbers 1, 20, 32, and 36 have been retired by the Philadelphia Phillies. For what players?

5. Who is the first man to be officially credited with breaking the four minute mile?

6. What three countries have each won three World Cups in soccer?

7. Name the three football coaches who have the most Division I-A coaching victories.

8. What tennis player made it to the finals of the U.S. Open Championship eight times in the 1980's?

9. Who hit the most home runs during the 1980's?

10. Who was the first man to regain the heavyweight title?

1. *They were the three horses with which he won the Kentucky Derby (in 1884, 1890, and 1891).*

2. *Ernie Nevers.*

3. *94 feet by 50 feet.*

4. *Number 1 - Richie Ashburn; Number 20 - Mike Schmidt; Number 32 - Steve Carlton; and Number 36 - Robin Roberts.*

5. *Roger Bannister of Great Britain, in 1954, with a time of 3:59.4.*

6. *Italy - 1934, 1938, and 1982; Brazil - 1958, 1962, and 1970; and West Germany - 1954, 1974, and 1990.*

7. *Paul "Bear" Bryant, 323; Amos Alonzo Stagg, 314; and Glenn "Pop" Warner, 313. (The reason that Eddie Robinson is not listed is because most of his victories came when Grambling was in Division I-AA.)*

8. *Ivan Lendl. He finished second in 1982, '83, '84, '88, and '89, and won in '85, '86, and '87.*

9. *Mike Schmidt - 313.*

10. *Floyd Patterson, who regained the title by kayoing Ingemar Johansson to whom he had lost the crown.*

1. After Muhammad Ali had his heavyweight title stripped from him, he did not fight for over three years. When he returned, he fought twice before facing Joe Frazier in Ali-Frazier I. What two boxers did he fight before tangling with Frazier?

2. Five different men have coached the Celtics to NBA Championships. How many can you get?

3. The Conn Smythe Trophy for Most Valuable Player during the NHL playoffs was first awarded in 1965. Only one player has won the Trophy two consecutive times. Who is he?

4. Who is Rocco Francis Marchegiano?

5. Who am I? In 1959, I played 152 games at second base for the Phillies and never played another game in the big leagues. My real first name is George.

6. Who is the first person to win more than one Olympic Marathon?

7. There are four cities that have won NBA Championships since 1947 which do not even have teams now. Name these cities.

8. Name one of the four players who have hit three homers in a game in each league.

9. Only three British golfers have won the British Open since 1952. Can you get two of them?

10. What two Major Leaguers have played all nine positions in a game?

4 Answers

1. *Jerry Quarry, whom he defeated by TKO in the third round; Oscar Bonavena, whom he defeated by TKO in the fifteenth round.*

2. *Red Auerbach, Bill Russell, Tommy Heinsohn, Bill Fitch, and K. C. Jones.*

3. *Bernie Parent of the Philadelphia Flyers, in 1973 and 1974.*

4. *Rocky Marciano.*

5. *Sparky Anderson.*

6. *Abebe Bikela of Ethiopia, in 1960 and 1964.*

7. *Baltimore, Rochester, Syracuse, and St. Louis.*

8. *Dave Kingman, Johnny Mize, Babe Ruth, and Claudell Washington.*

9. *Tony Jacklin, Sandy Lyle, and Nick Faldo.*

10. *Bert Campaneris, in 1964; Cesar Tovar, in 1968.*

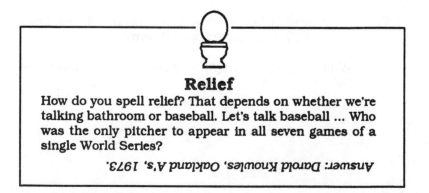

Relief

How do you spell relief? That depends on whether we're talking bathroom or baseball. Let's talk baseball ... Who was the only pitcher to appear in all seven games of a single World Series?

Answer: Darold Knowles, Oakland A's, 1973.

1. Paul "Bear" Bryant won 323 games as coach. At what four colleges did he win these games?

2. Name the three NFL teams which moved their homes at least 100 miles during the 1980's.

3. Who was the last Detroit Tiger to be the Junior Circuit's home run king?

4. What college football team has the most victories?

5. Who holds the record for the most consecutive free throws made in an NBA season?

6. Who's the only jockey to ride two horses to the Triple Crown?

7. In the second round of the 1977 Danny Thomas Classic, a PGA player shot the lowest tournament golf score for 18 holes. What was the score and who was the player?

8. Who was the last NBA leading scorer to play on a team that won the championship?

9. With what NFL team did Joe Namath end his career?

10. Who has the most World Series hits?

Answers

1. *Maryland (1945), Kentucky (1946-1953), Texas A&M (1954-1957), Alabama (1958-1982).*

2. *Raiders: Oakland to Los Angeles; Colts: Baltimore to Indianapolis; and Cardinals: St. Louis to Phoenix.*

3. *Cecil Fielder.*

4. *Michigan.*

5. *Calvin Murphy, with 78 in the 1980-1981 season.*

6. *Eddie Arcaro, who won with Whirlaway in 1941 and Citation in 1948.*

7. *Al Geiberger shot a 59.*

8. *Kareem Abdul-Jabbar, in 1971. At the time, he played for the Milwaukee Bucks under the name Lew Alcindor.*

9. *The Los Angeles Rams.*

10. *Yogi Berra, with 71.*

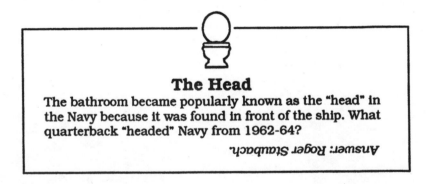

The Head
The bathroom became popularly known as the "head" in the Navy because it was found in front of the ship. What quarterback "headed" Navy from 1962-64?

Answer: Roger Staubach.

1. In 1974, Chris Evert was one of the top three money winners in two sports. What sports?

2. What NFL team won 17 consecutive Opening Day games?

3. Babe Ruth led the American League in homers while playing for the Yankees and also for the Red Sox. Can you name five other men who have led their leagues in home runs at least twice, playing for different teams each time?

4. What NBA team had a record of 9 and 73 one year?

5. Who am I? In 1961, I batted .361 to lead the league in hitting. In my other sixteen years in the Majors, I never batted over .286.

6. Only four different guards have been NBA MVP's. How many can you get?

7. What three non-Americans have won the U.S. Open Golf Championship in the past fifty years?

8. What Division I college basketball coach has the most victories?

9. In 1986, Red Sox pitcher Roger Clemens struck out twenty men to set a Major League record for a nine-inning game. Until then, the record had been held by three hurlers who fanned nineteen batters in a regulation contest. Who are they?

10. Since 1931, there have been three men having exactly four letters in their last names who have won National League MVP Awards. Name them.

1.   *Tennis and horse racing. The horse, Chris Evert, won over a half million dollars and was the top 3-year-old filly-of-the-year.*

2.   *The Dallas Cowboys, from 1965 to 1981.*

3.   *John Mize, New York Giants and St. Louis Cardinals; Dave Kingman, New York Mets and Chicago Cubs; Jimmy Foxx, Philadelphia A's and Boston Red Sox; Tony Armas, Oakland A's and Boston Red Sox; and Reggie Jackson, Oakland A's, New York Yankees, and California Angels.*

4.   *The 1972-73 Philadelphia 76ers.*

5.   *Norm Cash of the Detroit Tigers.*

6.   *Bob Cousy, Oscar Robertson, Magic Johnson, and Michael Jordan.*

7.   *Gary Player of South Africa, in 1965; Tony Jacklin of Great Britain, in 1970; and David Graham of Australia, in 1981.*

8.   *Adolph Rupp - 875.*

9.   *Steve Carlton of St. Louis, in 1969; Tom Seaver of the Mets, in 1970; Nolan Ryan of California, in 1974. (Carlton lost his game, 4-3, to the Mets on a pair of two-run homers by Ron Swoboda.)*

10. *Dizzy Dean, in 1934; Willie Mays, in 1954 and 1965; and Pete Rose, in 1973.*

1. Winter Olympics have been held in the United States three times. In which years and at what sites?

2. Buffalo has had three NBA Rookies of the Year. Name one of them.

3. Since 1940, only four American Leaguers have led their League in home runs for two consecutive years. Name these players. Hint: It happened exactly once in the 40's, 50's, 60's, and 70's.

4. Very few baseball players have exactly three letters in their last names. Name a Hall of Famer, an MVP, and a Rookie of the Year each having three letters in their last names.

5. The Jim Thorpe Trophy is awarded to the MVP of the NFL. What player won this award three consecutive times?

6. Who holds the Major League record for being hit by a pitch the most times during a season?

7. What two Division I college football teams have the nickname "Owls"?

8. In 1959, Elroy Face of the Pirates was 18-1 and did not win the Cy Young Award. Which National League pitcher did?

9. Name the two NHL teams which have won the most Stanley Cups.

10. Since 1950, only one player has had more than 150 RBI's in one season. Who? Hint: He played for 10 teams during his career.

1.   *Lake Placid, New York, 1932 and 1980; Squaw Valley, California, 1960.*

2.   *Bob McAdoo, 1973; Ernie DiGregorio, 1974; Adrian Dantley, 1977.*

3.   *Ted Williams, 1941, 1942; Mickey Mantle, 1955, 1956; Harmon Killebrew, 1962, 1963, 1964; Jim Rice, 1977, 1978.*

4.   *Hall of Famer - Mel Ott; MVP - Nellie Fox; Rookie of the Year - Steve Sax.*

5.   *Earl Campbell of Houston (in 1978, 1979, and 1980).*

6.   *Ron Hunt of Montreal, 50, in 1971.*

7.   *Rice and Temple.*

8.   *No National League pitcher did. Until 1966, only one Cy Young Award was given out between the two Leagues. The winner in 1959 was Early Wynn of the Chicago White Sox, who was 22-10.*

9.   *Montreal Canadians, 22, and the Toronto Maple Leafs, 11.*

10.   *Tommy Davis, who drove home 153 runs in 1962.*

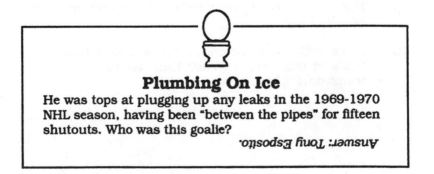

Plumbing On Ice
He was tops at plugging up any leaks in the 1969-1970 NHL season, having been "between the pipes" for fifteen shutouts. Who was this goalie?

Answer: Tony Esposito.

1. What player was on deck when both Hank Aaron and Sadaharu Oh each got his 715th home run?

2. There have been five Heisman Trophy winners from Army and Navy. Who are they?

3. Name one of the three NFL teams for which Don Shula played.

4. Who knocked in the most runs during the 1980's?

5. Name the only person to win both Rookie of the Year and Coach of the Year Awards in the NBA.

6. Who is the only American man in the last 75 years to win the marathon in the Olympics?

7. What college basketball team holds the record for consecutive wins? What team ended the streak?

8. What is the name for the machine which cleans the ice between periods at an NHL hockey game?

9. Who was the first Major Leaguer to have been caught stealing twice in the same inning? Hint: He's also hit more homers as a designated hitter than any other player.

10. Name the horses which have won the Kentucky Derby twice.

1. *Davey Johnson. He was with the Braves in the National League when Aaron did it and was a teammate of Oh's in the Japanese League when he did it.*

2. *Army: Doc Blanchard, 1945; Glenn Davis, 1946; Pete Dawkins, 1958. Navy: Joe Bellino, 1960; Roger Staubach, 1963.*

3. *Cleveland Browns, Baltimore Colts, and Washington Redskins.*

4. *Eddie Murray - 996.*

5. *Tommy Heinsohn. In 1956-57, he was Rookie of the Year with Boston and, in 1973, won Coach of the Year for the Celtics.*

6. *Frank Shorter, at the 1972 Olympic Games held in Munich.*

7. *UCLA - they won 88 consecutive games in the early 1970's. Notre Dame beat them to end the streak.*

8. *A Zamboni (named for its inventor).*

9. *Don Baylor.*

10. *No horse has ever won the Kentucky Derby twice. The race is only for three-year-olds.*

1. Only four forwards have won NBA MVP Awards. Name three of them.

2. Secretariat won the Triple Crown in 1973. The previous Triple Crown winner won 25 years earlier. Which horse did it?

3. In the first Super Bowl game, two players scored rushing touchdowns. Who were they?

4. As a professional, Muhammad Ali lost five fights. Name the men who defeated him.

5. Name the two NHL goalies who have scored goals.

6. Since 1911, only two players have led their leagues in home runs hitting the same number as the year. Chuck Klein hit 31 in '31. Who was the other player to do this?

7. Since 1896, Summer Olympics have been held in three cities that begin with the letter "A". Name these cities.

8. In the 1962 World Series, a former Yankee pitcher won a game against the Yankees while pitching for the Giants. Name him.

9. What is the highest possible score in bowling if you never throw two strikes in a row?

10. In 1974, a player won the U.S. Open Tennis Chamionship by scores of 6-1, 6-0, 6-1. Who won and whom did he defeat?

1.   Bob Pettit, Julius Erving, Bob McAdoo, and Larry Bird.

2.   Citation.

3.   In the first half of an eventual 35-10 Green Bay Packer victory over the Kansas City Chiefs, Jim Taylor of the Packers scored on a 14-yard run. In the second half, Elijah Pitts scored two more rushing touchdowns for the Pack. The other 24 points were scored on three passing touchdowns and a Kansas City field goal.

4.   Joe Frazier, Ken Norton, Leon Spinks, Larry Holmes, and Trevor Berbick.

5.   Billy Smith of the Islanders and Ron Hextall of the Flyers. In reality, only Hextall actually shot the puck into the net. Smith was given credit for a goal when an opponent shot the puck into his own net.

6.   Roger Maris, with 61 in '61. It's safe to assume that there won't be another answer to this question for approximately 40 years.

7.   Athens (1896), Antwerp (1920), and Amsterdam (1928).

8.   Don Larsen.

9.   200.

10.   Jimmy Connors defeated Ken Rosewall.

1. During the 1980's, six brothers from the same family played in the NHL. Give their last name.

2. Who's the oldest man to hit a Major League grand slam?

3. From 1971 to 1980, Jack Nicklaus and Tom Watson were the leading money winners on the PGA Tour every year except one, 1974. Who led that year? Hint: He is a Mormon.

4. The biggest margin of victory in an NCAA Basketball Championship Game is 30 points. Name the winning and losing teams in the contest.

5. Name the three Hispanic players who have won the Cy Young Award.

6. What player won the U.S. Men's Tennis Championship exactly twice, with a gap of fourteen years between championships?

7. What team holds the NBA record for consecutive wins?

8. Can you name the five starters on this record-setting team?

9. What three men have played the most games in goal in the NHL?

10. What were the real first names of the following stars of the Yankees: Yogi Berra, Whitey Ford, Mickey Mantle?

Answers

1. Sutter. Their given names are Brent, Brian, Darryl, Duane, Rich, and Ron.

2. Tony Perez of the Reds, who did it in 1985 when he was 42 years old.

3. Johnny Miller.

4. UNLV beat Duke, 103-73, in the 1990 Championship Game.

5. Mike Cuellar, 1969; Fernando Valenzuela, 1981; and Willie Hernandez, 1984.

6. Ken Rosewall, in 1956 and 1970.

7. The Los Angeles Lakers of the early '70's, who won 33 consecutive games.

8. Center - Wilt Chamberlain; Forwards - Happy Hairston and Jim McMillan; Guards - Jerry West and Gail Goodrich.

9. Terry Sawchuk - 971; Glenn Hall - 906; and Tony Esposito - 886.

10. Lawrence Berra, Edward Ford, Mickey Mantle.

Bathroom All-Star Stuff

It's the manufacturer of a men's bathroom product and for many years was the sponsor of baseball's All-Star balloting. Name the company.

Answer: Gillette.

1.   What five men have played for and managed the Mets?

2.   Since 1924, what four countries have won gold medals in ice hockey in the Olympics?

3.   Only twice has a country won soccer's World Cup while playing outside its own continent. Name one of these countries.

4.   What pitcher has the record for striking out the most batters in a game?

5.   Who's the only American in the last 50 years to hold the world's record for the mile run?

6.   The 1982 NCAA Championship Game between North Carolina and Georgetown featured six players who were first or second round NBA draft choices. How many can you get?

7.   Only one National League player has ever hit two grand slam home runs in a game. Who did it and what makes the feat even more unusual?

8.   Only three fillies have ever won the Kentucky Derby. Name one of them.

9.   Name the three men who have played the most games for the Dodgers.

10. What Wimbledon champion has a brother who played Major League baseball?

1. *Gil Hodges, Yogi Berra, Roy McMillan, Joe Torre, and Bud Harrelson.*

2. *Canada, U.S.S.R., the United States, and Great Britain. Great Britain won the Gold Medal in 1936.*

3. *Brazil, in 1958, when the World Cup was held in Sweden, and Argentina, in 1986, when it was held in Mexico.*

4. *Tom Cheney of Washington, who struck out 21 batters in a 16-inning game in 1962.*

5. *Jim Ryun, who held the record from 1966 to 1975.*

6. *North Carolina: Michael Jordan, James Worthy, and Sam Perkins; Georgetown: Patrick Ewing, Eric Floyd, and Bill Martin.*

7. *Tony Cloninger of Atlanta, in 1966. What makes the feat extraordinary is that he was a pitcher.*

8. *Regret, in 1915; Genuine Risk, in 1980; and Winning Colors, in 1988.*

9. *Zack Wheat, Pee Wee Reese, and Bill Russell.*

10. *Billie Jean King. Her brother Randy Moffit pitched in the Majors during the 1970's and 1980's.*

1. Ralph Kiner led the National League in home runs seven consecutive years. In three of these years, he actually tied for the lead. With what players?

2. Name the two jockeys who have won the Kentucky Derby five times.

3. What golfer once won eleven consecutive tournaments?

4. Four different Orioles have won the Cy Young Award. Who are they?

5. Duke and Kansas are two of three teams which have lost the NCAA Basketball Championship Final Game four times. Can you name the third four-time loser?

6. Jim Brown led the NFL in rushing every year from 1957 to 1965 except for one year. What player broke his streak?

7. Which four American League stadiums have artificial grass?

8. In Olympic Figure Skating, who is the only woman to win a gold medal in Women's Singles more than twice?

9. In tennis, what four events comprise the modern Grand Slam?

10. There are five Hall of Famers who have played in the Majors since 1950 who have exactly four letters in their last names. Who are they?

1. *John Mize, in 1947 and 1948; Hank Sauer, in 1952.*

2. *Eddie Arcaro, in 1938, 1941, 1945, 1948, and 1952; Bill Hartack, in 1957, 1960, 1962, 1964, and 1969.*

3. *Byron Nelson, in 1945.*

4. *Mike Cuellar, in 1969; Jim Palmer, in 1973, 1975, and 1976; Mike Flanagan, in 1979; Steve Stone, in 1980.*

5. *North Carolina, (1946, 1968, 1977, and 1981).*

6. *Jim Taylor of Green Bay, in 1962.*

7. *Kansas City, Minnesota, Seattle, and Toronto.*

8. *Sonja Henie of Norway, in 1928, 1932, and 1936.*

9. *Wimbledon and the Australian, French and U.S. Opens.*

10. *Whitey Ford, George Kell, Willie Mays, John Mize, and Early Wynn.*

1. Of all the heavyweight championship fights of this century, which had the smallest attendance?

2. Two National Leaguers hold the record for most home runs hit in a day, five. Name one of these players.

3. What best-selling author who received more than 75,000 votes in the Presidential Election of 1972, won a gold medal in the 1924 Olympics?

4. The nickname "Giants" is shared by the NFL NY Giants and the Major League Baseball San Francisco Giants. If we restrict ourselves to the NFL, NHL, NBA and Major League Baseball, there are five other nicknames shared by two teams. What are they?

5. Who is the only player in the 1980's to play in both the NBA and in Major League Baseball?

6. In the ten year period, 1954-1963, the Yankees had the MVP eight times. Name the two American League non-Yankees who won MVP.

7. What is the record for the most batters struck out by a pitcher in an inning? Theoretically, what is the most number of strikeouts which a pitcher can get in an inning?

8. Two Hall of Famers who played in the 1970's never played in a World Series or even made a League Championship Series. They were teammates for six years. Name one of them.

9. What former gold medal-winning athlete lit the Olympic flame at the start of the 1984 Summer Olympics at Los Angeles?

10. Who was the last Cleveland Indian to lead the American League in homers?

1. The second Sonny Liston-Cassius Clay fight, which was held in Lewiston, Maine, in 1965. Less than three thousand people attended the fight.

2. Stan Musial of the St. Louis Cardinals and Nate Colbert of the San Diego Padres. Each hit his five homers in a doubleheader.

3. Benjamin Spock. He won his gold medal in rowing.

4. Rangers: Texas baseball and New York hockey; Oilers: Houston football and Edmonton hockey; Jets: New York football and Winnipeg hockey; Cardinals: Phoenix football and St. Louis baseball; Kings: Los Angeles hockey and Sacramento basketball.

5. Danny Ainge, who played baseball for the Toronto Blue Jays and basketball for the Boston Celtics and Sacramento Kings.

6. Jackie Jensen of the Boston Red Sox, in 1958; Nellie Fox of the Chicago White Sox, in 1959.

7. The record for most strikeouts in an inning by a pitcher is four, held by many players. Theoretically, there is no limit to the number of strikeouts which a pitcher can get in an inning since, when there are two outs or when first base is unoccupied, a batter may run to first if the third strike gets past the catcher.

8. Ernie Banks and Ferguson Jenkins.

9. Rafer Johnson of the United States, who won the gold medal in the Decathlon at the 1960 Summer Olympics, held in Rome.

10. Rocky Colavito, in 1959.

1. Name two Oscar Award-winning movies about sports.

2. What man played in every Brooklyn Dodger-New York Yankee World Series game?

3. In what entire World Series did only nine players bat for one team? Who were the nine players?

4. Who was the youngest woman to win a Singles Championship in the U.S. Open Tennis Championships?

5. Who has won the Indianapolis 500 the most times?

6. Who is the only player to hit home runs for four different Major League teams in the same season?

7. What person has won more games than any other pitcher whose last name begins with the letter "O"?

8. Who is Edson Arantes do Nascimento?

9. There have been three goalies who have won the Vezina Trophy for two different teams. Name one.

10. Two men managed for over twenty years apiece and never won a pennant. Give one of them.

1. Rocky *(in 1976)* and Chariots of Fire *(in 1981).*

2. *Pee Wee Reese.*

3. *The Cincinnati Reds did this in the 1976 World Series which they swept from the New York Yankees. Since the designated hitter was in use during that Series, no pitcher batted for the Reds. The nine men who did bat were: Pete Rose (3B), Joe Morgan (2B), Ken Griffey (RF), Johnny Bench (C), George Foster (LF), Dave Concepcion (SS), Tony Perez (1B), Dan Driessen (DH), and Cesar Geronimo (CF).*

4. *Tracy Austin, in 1979.*

5. *A. J. Foyt, Jr., Al Unser, and Rick Mears; each won it four times.*

6. *Dave Kingman, in 1977. He hit them for the New York Mets, California Angels, San Diego Padres and the New York Yankees.*

7. *Claude Osteen, who won 196.*

8. *Pele.*

9. *Glenn Hall-Chicago and St. Louis; Jacques Plante-Montreal and St. Louis; Terry Sawchuk-Toronto and Detroit.*

10. *Jimmy Dykes and Gene Mauch.*

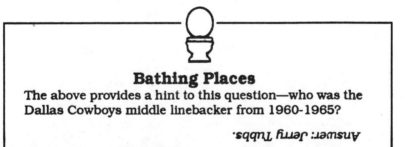

Bathing Places

The above provides a hint to this question—who was the Dallas Cowboys middle linebacker from 1960-1965?

Answer: Jerry Tubbs.

1. In the 1981 strike-shortened baseball season, what team won the most games but did not even participate in the playoffs?

2. Man O'War lost only one horse race. What horse upset him?

3. What former NFL player held the world record for the 100-yard dash?

4. Who is the only undefeated horse to win the Kentucky Derby? Hint: He was a Triple Crown winner.

5. Who played goal for the 1980 gold medal-winning U.S. Olympic hockey team?

6. What NBA coach has the most career victories? Give his real first name.

7. What pitcher holds the record for the most consecutive wins?

8. Besides John Wooden, name two of the four men to coach consecutive winners of NCAA Division I Basketball Championships.

9. Wooden, of course, won his Championships with UCLA. Can you name the schools with which each of the other four coaches won?

10. Joe Frazier entered the 1964 Olympic Games as a replacement for what boxer who had to withdraw because of an injury?

1. *The Cincinnati Reds.*

2. *Coincidentally, a horse named Upset.*

3. *Bob Hayes, 9.1 seconds.*

4. *Seattle Slew, in 1977.*

5. *Jim Craig. (Steve Janaszak was the second goalie for the United States but did not appear in an Olympic game.)*

6. *Arnold "Red" Auerbach.*

7. *Carl Hubbell, who won 24 straight games over a two-year period.*

8. *Hank Iba, Adolph Rupp, Phil Woolpert, and Ed Jucker.*

9. *Iba: Oklahoma A & M - 1945 and '46; Rupp: Kentucky - 1948 and '49; Woolpert: San Francisco - 1955 and '56; and Jucker: Cincinnati - 1961 and '62.*

10. *Buster Mathis.*

1. Who was the Manassa Mauler?

2. In the 1934 All-Star Game, Carl Hubbell struck out five future Hall of Famers in succession. Who were they?

3. Who was the first woman to be named Athlete of the Year by *Sports Illustrated*?

4. Since 1960, only one NFL player has scored six touchdowns in a game. Who?

5. Who was the only man to manage a Major League baseball game and to be the skipper of an America's Cup yacht winner?

6. Who holds the Major League record for runs batted in in a season?

7. To the nearest foot, what is the distance from homeplate to second base: 120 feet, 123 feet, or 127 feet?

8. Who is Cornelius McGillicuddy?

9. Muhammad Ali won the heavyweight title three times. Name the men he defeated.

10. What NFL quarterback holds the record for the most consecutive passing attempts without an interception?

1. *Jack Dempsey.*

2. *Babe Ruth, Lou Gehrig, Jimmy Foxx, Al Simmons, and Joe Cronin.*

3. *Billie Jean King, in 1972.*

4. *Gale Sayers, in 1965.*

5. *Ted Turner. He was the skipper of the Courageous when it won America's Cup in 1977 and he managed the Atlanta Braves (the team which he owns) for one game. By the way, he lost the game.*

6. *Hack Wilson of the Cubs, who knocked in 190 runs in 1930.*

7. *127 feet.*

8. *Connie Mack.*

9. *Sonny Liston, George Foreman, and Leon Spinks. Just in case you were thinking that "Frazier" was an answer, Smokin' Joe was not the champ when Ali defeated him.*

10. *Bart Starr of Green Bay, who threw 294 consecutive passes during the 1964 and 1965 seasons without being intercepted.*

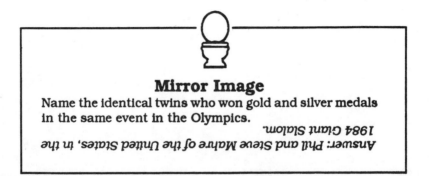

Mirror Image

Name the identical twins who won gold and silver medals in the same event in the Olympics.

Answer: Phil and Steve Mahre of the United States, in the 1984 Giant Slalom.

1. There have been three men who won National League Rookie of the Year honors and later led the American League in home runs. Can you come up with them?

2. Bob Cousy and Bill Sharman were two of the top guards in the NBA when they played for the Celtics during the 50's. What colleges did they attend?

3. What American was voted United States' Athlete of the Half-Century for the first part of the Twentieth Century? What Canadian was voted Canada's Athlete of the Half-Century?

4. What Division I-A football team had the longest winning streak? What college defeated them to end the streak?

5. Which of the following men holds the record for the most consecutive seasons playing 150 or more games — Hank Aaron, Lou Gehrig, Willie Mays, or Pete Rose?

6. What did Bobo Holloman of the St. Louis Browns do in his first Major League start?

7. Name the first American club to join the NHL.

8. True or False: When he was a teenager growing up in Baltimore, Babe Ruth competed as a jockey in the Preakness.

9. What NFL teams play their home games in the following locations — Irving, Foxboro and Pontiac?

10. In the 1970's, three American League MVP's had exactly four letters in their last names. You should be able to get all three of them.

1. *Frank Robinson won Rookie of the Year in 1956 with the Reds, and led the American League in home runs in 1966 with the Orioles; Frank Howard was top rookie with the Dodgers in 1960, and led the AL in 1968 and 1970 with the Washington Senators; Richie Allen was NL Rookie of the Year with the Phillies in 1964, and won the home run title with the White Sox in 1972 and 1974.*

2. *Cousy - Holy Cross; Sharman - USC.*

3. *United States - Jim Thorpe; Canada - Lionel "Big Train" Conacher.*

4. *From 1953 through 1957, Oklahoma University won 47 straight games. The streak was broken in 1957 by Notre Dame, who defeated the Bud Wilkerson-led Sooners, 7 to 0.*

5. *Willie Mays, who did it in thirteen consecutive seasons. (In 1935, the Yankees played only 149 games. Even though Gehrig played in all of them, it prevented him from sharing this record. Pete Rose probably would have set the record with fifteen consecutive seasons but the 1981 strike made playing 150 games impossible.)*

6. *He pitched a no-hitter.*

7. *The Boston Bruins, in 1924.*

8. *False.*

9. *Irving - Dallas Cowboys; Foxboro - New England Patriots; Pontiac - Detroit Lions.*

10. *Vida Blue, in 1971; Fred Lynn, in 1975; Jim Rice, in 1978.*

1. Al Michaels and Dan Dierdoff are the newest additions to the Monday Night Football announcing staff. There have been nine other men behind the mike. How many do you know?

2. The 1971 Orioles had four pitchers win twenty or more games apiece. Name them.

3. Who was the winning pitcher in the longest World Series game?

4. True or False: Brooke Shields' grandfather lost in the finals for the U.S. Singles Tennis Championship.

5. Who was the first NHL goalie to regularly wear a mask when he played?

6. Harry Boykoff, a 6'9" All-American at St. John's, was one of the players who helped cause the introduction of what new rule in the 1944-1945 college basketball season?

7. New York Yankee Don Mattingly homered in eight consecutive games in 1987. Whose record did he tie?

8. What heavyweight boxing champion had a brother who pitched in the Majors?

9. What Supreme Court Justice was once the leading rusher in the NFL?

10. Only counting players who had gotten up enough times to qualify for the batting title, list all the American League players who batted above .290 in 1968.

1.   *Howard Cosell, Keith Jackson, Don Meredith, Frank Gifford, Fred Williamson, Alex Karras, Fran Tarkenton, O.J. Simpson, and Joe Namath.*

2.   *Dave McNally had 21 wins. Mike Cuellar, Pat Dobson, and Jim Palmer each had 20.*

3.   *Babe Ruth of the Boston Red Sox, in 1916. He pitched a fourteen-inning complete game to beat the Brooklyn Dodgers, 2-1.*

4.   *True. Frank Shields was one of the top tennis players of the time and, in 1930, made it to the final round of the U.S. Tennis Championships before losing.*

5.   *Jacques Plante of the Montreal Canadians.*

6.   *Goaltending.*

7.   *Dale Long of the Pittsburgh Pirates.*

8.   *Jim Corbett. His brother Joe pitched for four years in the National League. In 1897, he was 24-8 for the Baltimore team.*

9.   *Byron "Whizzer" White.*

10.   *There was only one — Carl Yastrzemski of Boston, who won the batting title with a .301 average. Danny Cater finished second with a .290 average.*

1. "A player cannot run with the ball. The player must throw it from the spot on which he catches it; allowance to be made for a man who catches the ball while running at a good speed." This was one of the original rules of what sport?

2. There have been two American League players to have driven in one hundred or more runs for thirteen consecutive seasons. Name these players.

3. What team did Al McGuire coach to an NCAA basketball title?

4. In the 1972 Team Canada — Russia Series, eight hockey games were played. How many games did each win?

5. Do you know the two players who have gotten one hundred or more hits batting left-handed and one hundred or more hits batting right-handed in the same season?

6. Who was the last British woman to win the Singles Title at Wimbledon? How about the last British man to win the Singles at Wimbledon?

7. Is it possible for a team to get six hits in an inning and not score a run?

8. In 1990, UCLA retired basketball numbers 32 and 33. For what players?

9. What two NFL teams have helmets on their helmets?

10. Who was the first man to hit a grand slam home run in an All-Star Game?

1.   *Basketball.*

2.   *Lou Gehrig, who did it from 1926 to 1938; Jimmie Foxx, who did it from 1929 to 1941.*

3.   *Marquette.*

4.   *Canada won four, Russia won three, and there was one tie.*

5.   *Garry Templeton and Willie Wilson.*

6.   *Woman: Virginia Wade, in 1977; Man: Fred Perry, in 1936.*

7.   *Yes. The key is to have the third out of the inning made by a ground ball which hits a runner — this is counted as an out for the team, but a hit for the batter.*

8.   *Bill Walton, 32; Kareem Abdul-Jabbar, 33. (Note: Abdul-Jabbar played under the name Lew Alcindor while at UCLA.)*

9.   *The Los Angeles Raiders and the Miami Dolphins.*

10.   *Fred Lynn, in 1983.*

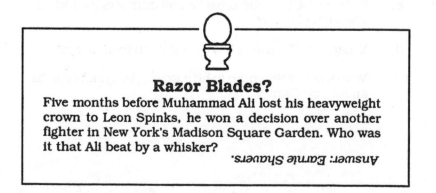

Razor Blades?

Five months before Muhammad Ali lost his heavyweight crown to Leon Spinks, he won a decision over another fighter in New York's Madison Square Garden. Who was it that Ali beat by a whisker?

Answer: Earnie Shavers.

1. What four NFL teams have bird nicknames?

2. Who was the first black man to play in the NBA?

3. What colleges did Magic Johnson and Larry Bird attend?

4. In 1987 and 1988, Baltimore Orioles skipper Cal Ripkin enjoyed the distinction of being father and manager to his sons, Cal, Jr., and Billy. In the history of baseball, three other managers have had their sons on their teams. Who are they?

5. Who am I? In June, 1988, I appeared on the covers of *Time, Life, People,* and *Sports Illustrated.*

6. What American Leaguer holds the record for the most grand slam homers? What National Leaguer holds the Senior Circuit's record?

7. Three of the backfield stars of the 1960's Green Bay Packers were Bart Starr, Jim Taylor, and Paul Hornung. Name the colleges which these three men went to.

8. On April 11, 1954, the Yankees acquired future Hall of Famer Enos Slaughter from the Cardinals for three players. One of these players became the National League Rookie of the Year in 1955 and later became a Yankee manager. Who is he?

9. The first Monday Night Football Game was held in 1970. Do you know the teams that played?

10. Who am I? My real first name is Forrest. I participated in over 500 baseball games in which I did not play a defensive position although I was never a designated hitter. I also played over a thousand other games at a single defensive position.

1. *Atlanta Falcons, Phoenix Cardinals, Seattle Seahawks, and Philadelphia Eagles.*

2. *Chuck Cooper of the Boston Celtics.*

3. *Magic Johnson - Michigan State; Larry Bird - Indiana and Indiana State.*

4. *Connie Mack managed his son, Earle, with the Philadelphia Athletics in 1910, 1911, and 1914. Yogi Berra managed his son, Dale, with the New York Yankees at the beginning of the 1985 season until Yogi was fired. And, Hal McRae managed his son, Brian, with the 1991 Kansas City Royals.*

5. *Mike Tyson.*

6. *American - Lou Gehrig, with 23; National - Willie McCovey, with 18.*

7. *Starr - Alabama; Taylor - Louisiana State; Hornung -Notre Dame.*

8. *Bill Virdon.*

9. *New York Jets and Cleveland Browns.*

10. *Smokey Burgess.*

1. What three NHL teams play their home games within 40 miles of each other?

2. The Outland Trophy is awarded each year to the outstanding lineman in college football. The 1957 winner, who played for Iowa, and the 1961 winner, who played for Utah State, each later became a star of a television series in the 1980's. Name these players.

3. Who was the first designated hitter to hit a regular season home run? How about the first DH to hit a World Series round tripper?

4. What NFL team drafted Bo Jackson first in the nation?

5. What NBA forward was named First Team All-Star for ten consecutive seasons?

6. There have been four players who have pitched more than two-hundred innings in a season before the age of twenty. How many can you think of?

7. True or False: Someone has played Major League baseball and in the Super Bowl.

8. The football Giants have played their home games in three states. Name them.

9. A 1970's American League home run leader had two brothers play in the Majors in a year in which he led in home runs. Who is this slugger?

10. In the 1972 World Series, what player hit home runs in his first two at-bats?

1. *New York Rangers, New York Islanders, and New Jersey Devils.*

2. *1957: Alex Karras; 1961: Merlin Olsen.*

3. *Regular season: Tony Oliva of the Minnesota Twins, in 1973; World Series: Dan Driessen of the Cincinnati Reds, in 1976.*

4. *Tampa Bay Buccaneers.*

5. *Bob Pettit, from the 1954-1955 season to the 1963-1964 season.*

6. *Bob Feller of the Cleveland Indians, in 1938; Wally Bunker of the Baltimore Orioles, in 1964; Gary Nolan of the Cincinnati Reds, in 1967; Dwight Gooden of the New York Mets, in 1984.*

7. *True. Tom Brown played 61 games for the Washington Senators, in 1963, and played for the Green Bay Packers in the first two Super Bowls.*

8. *New York: Polo Grounds and Yankee Stadium; Connecticut: Yale Bowl; New Jersey: Giants Stadium.*

9. *In 1972, Richie Allen of the Chicago White Sox hit 37 home runs to lead the American League. That same year, his brother Hank played nine games with the White Sox and his brother Ron played nine games with the Cardinals. (Joe DiMaggio's two brothers did not play in the Majors in the two years in which DiMaggio led the American League in homers.)*

10. *Gene Tenace.*

1. The 1961 New York Yankees hit a record 240 home runs. The Yanks had seven men hit ten or more homers that year. How many can you name?

2. Name the two boxers who knocked down Muhammad Ali during championship fights.

3. Who is the youngest player ever elected to the Baseball Hall of Fame?

4. Who has the most lifetime home runs of all those players who never led their league in home runs?

5. Who am I? I gained 10,000 rushing yards in 91 NFL games, faster than any other player.

6. Name the defensive front four of the Pittsburgh Steelers who played in Super Bowls IX and X.

7. Since 1950, which Major League baseball teams have played their home games in Milwaukee? Hint: There are three clubs.

8. Only one NFL player has ever had two TD runs of over 90 yards in his career. Can you think of him?

9. Two trainers have had two Triple Crown winners in thoroughbred racing. Name one of them.

10. Name the one-time National League MVP who played over five hundred games at catcher, first base, and third base.

1. *Roger Maris, 61; Mickey Mantle, 54; Bill "Moose" Skowron, 28; Yogi Berra, 22; Elston Howard, 21; John Blanchard, 21; Clete Boyer, 11.*

2. *Joe Frazier and Chuck Wepner.*

3. *Sandy Koufax, who was 35 when he was elected in 1971.*

4. *Stan Musial, 475.*

5. *Eric Dickerson.*

6. *Joe Green, L.C. Greenwood, Ernie Holmes, and Dwight White.*

7. *The Milwaukee Braves, the Milwaukee Brewers, and the Chicago White Sox. In 1968 and 1969, the White Sox played one game per season in Milwaukee against each one of their opponents.*

8. *Bo Jackson. He had a 91-yard run in 1987 and a 92-yarder in 1989.*

9. *"Sunny Jim" Fitzsimmons: Gallant Fox (1930) and Omaha (1935); Ben Jones: Whirlaway (1941) and Citation (1948).*

10. *Joe Torre.*

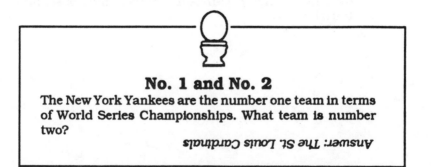

No. 1 and No. 2

The New York Yankees are the number one team in terms of World Series Championships. What team is number two?

Answer: The St. Louis Cardinals

1. There have been four Heisman Trophy winners having exactly four letters in their last names. Who are they?

2. What two pitchers have won thirty or more games in a season more than twice?

3. Who am I? In December, 1989, three months after signing what was then the richest contract in NFL history, I kicked a 91-yard punt - the third longest NFL punt of all time.

4. What are the dimensions and shape of a hockey net? What are the dimensions and shape of a basketball hoop?

5. The 1963 Dodgers swept the Yankees using only four pitchers. Who were they?

6. Who were the only brothers to win league batting championships? Name the only two brothers to finish one-two in batting during a season.

7. Name the NBA guard who was a First Team All Star for ten consecutive seasons.

8. Name the only NFL team not to have an emblem on its helmet.

9. What player played the most games for the Yankees?

10. During the 1970's what unusual feat did both Cesar Gutierrez and Rennie Stennett accomplish?

1. *Leon Hart of Notre Dame, in 1949; John David Crow of Texas A & M, in 1957; Billy Sims of Oklahoma, in 1978; and Andre Ware of Houston, in 1989.*

2. *Christy Mathewson - four times (in 1903, 1904, 1905, and 1908); Grover Cleveland Alexander - three times (in 1915, 1916, and 1917).*

3. *Randall Cunningham of the Eagles.*

4. *Hockey net: a rectangle which is four feet by six feet; Basketball hoop: a circle with a diameter of seventeen and three-quarter inches.*

5. *Sandy Koufax, Don Drysdale, Johnny Podres, and Ron Perranoski.*

6. *The only brothers to win batting championships are Harry and Dixie Walker. Harry Walker did it in 1947, when playing for the St. Louis Cardinals and the Philadelphia Phillies; Dixie Walker did it in 1944, for the Brooklyn Dodgers. The only two brothers to finish one-two in batting were the Alous, Matty and Felipe, in 1966. Matty, who won, played for the Pirates; Felipe played for the Atlanta Braves.*

7. *Bob Cousy, from the 1951-1952 season to the 1960-1961 season.*

8. *The Cleveland Browns.*

9. *Mickey Mantle, with 2401 regular season games.*

10. *They both got seven hits in game. Gutierrez went seven-for-seven in a 1970 extra-inning game, while playing for the Tigers; Stennett went seven-for-seven in a 1975 nine-inning game, while playing for the Pirates.*

1. In 1986, Mike Schmidt won the National League MVP Award for the third time (he won back-to-back honors in 1980 and 1981). There were two other three-time MVP's in the National League. Can you name either one?

2. What team won the first ABA Championship, in the 1967-1968 season?

3. There has been only one perfect game pitched in World Series history. Name the year, the two teams, the final score, the winning and losing pitchers, and the final two batters.

4. The New York Yankees have played their home games at three stadiums. Name them.

5. True or False: The U.S. Olympic Team did not win a single gold medal during the 1980 Summer Olympics.

6. Since 1950, four NHL players have won MVP Awards more than twice. Who are the four players?

7. What American Leaguer has played the most games at shortstop? What National Leaguer?

8. How many minutes in a half in a pro basketball game? College basketball game? High school basketball game?

9. Who was the only baseball player to have played in the Majors during the 1940's, 1950's, 1960's, 1970's, and 1980's?

10. Who was an NFL coach for forty seasons?

1. *Stan Musial of the St. Louis Cardinals, in 1943, 1946, and 1948; Roy Campanella of the Brooklyn Dodgers, in 1951, 1953, and 1955.*

2. *The Pittsburgh Pipers, who defeated the New Orleans Buccaneers.*

3. *Year: 1956; teams: New York Yankees and Brooklyn Dodgers; final score: 2-0 Yankees; winning pitcher: Don Larsen; losing pitcher: Sal Maglie; final two batters: Roy Campanella and Dale Mitchell.*

4. *Polo Grounds, Yankee Stadium, and Shea Stadium.*

5. *True. The United States team boycotted the 1980 Olympics, which was held in Moscow.*

6. *Gordie Howe, Bobby Orr, Bobby Clarke, and Wayne Gretzky.*

7. *American Leaguer: Luis Aparicio; National Leaguer: Larry Bowa.*

8. *Pro: twenty-four; College: twenty; High School: sixteen.*

9. *Minnie Minoso. He played from 1949 to 1964 but, as a gimmick, got up eight times in 1976, at the age of 53, and got up twice in 1980, at the age of 57. He got one hit in 1976 and no hits in 1980. The White Sox petitioned the Commissioner's Office in 1990 to permit Minoso to bat during the 1990 season but were turned down.*

10. *George Halas.*

1. Who were the first five men elected to the Baseball Hall of Fame?

2. Since 1950, the Dodgers have played their home games at four different stadiums. How many can you name?

3. The first NFL game played outside of North America was held in what country? Hint: It was a pre-season game.

4. Name the only college to win both the NCAA and the NIT Basketball Championships in the same season.

5. What pitcher holds the record for consecutive shutout innings in World Series play and whose record did he break?

6. Who is the only man in the Pro Football, College Football and Baseball Halls of Fame?

7. Three colleges which begin with the letter "L" have been NCAA Basketball Champions. Give all three.

8. The 1949 Boston Red Sox had two players knock in 159 runs apiece that season. Who were these players?

9. Six new teams entered the NHL for the 1967-1968 season. Can you name all of them?

10. Who am I? I'm the only player to play over five hundred games with each of four different teams.

1. *Ty Cobb, Babe Ruth, Honus Wagner, Christy Math-ewson, and Walter Johnson.*

2. *Ebbets Field, Brooklyn; Roosevelt Stadium, Jersey City; Los Angeles Coliseum; Dodger Stadium (previously known as Chavez Ravine), Los Angeles.*

3. *Japan, in 1976. The St. Louis Cardinals beat the San Diego Chargers in an exhibition game.*

4. *C.C.N.Y. (City College of New York), which won the 1950 Championships.*

5. *Whitey Ford of the Yankees holds the record with 32 consecutive shutout innings. Ford broke the record previously held by Boston Red Sox left-hander, Babe Ruth. Ruth's record was 29⅔ innings.*

6. *Cal Hubbard.*

7. *LaSalle - 1954; Loyola of Chicago - 1963; and Louisville - 1980 and 1986.*

8. *Ted Williams and Vern Stephens.*

9. *Los Angeles Kings, Minnesota North Stars, Pittsburgh Penguins, Philadelphia Flyers, Oakland Seals, and St. Louis Blues.*

10. *Rusty Staub. He did it with the Astros, Expos, Mets, and Tigers.*

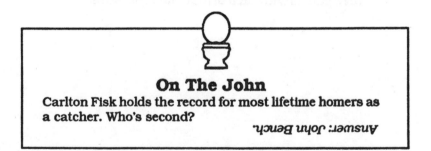

On The John
Carlton Fisk holds the record for most lifetime homers as a catcher. Who's second?

Answer: John Bench.

1. Name the three men who defeated Joe Louis when he was a professional.

2. Since 1940, only one man has led the league in batting at different times playing for different teams. Who?

3. What draft choice of the Cleveland Browns had his number retired by the team although he never played a game for them?

4. Who am I? I played in over one hundred regular season games and I played three World Series games. I'm not a pitcher and I never went to bat in the Majors.

5. Who holds the American League consecutive game hitting streak? How many games? Who holds the National League record? How many games?

6. What college was the first to field a men's basketball team?

7. Certain pitchers are known for giving up famous home runs. Identify the famous homer which each of the following pitchers gave up — Al Downing, Tracy Stallard, Tom Zachary.

8. True or False: During the 1920's, there were a Pittsburgh Pirates baseball team and a Pittsburgh Pirates National Hockey League team.

9. If two football teams play a game and score a total of less than thirty points, what is the most unlikely final score?

10. The 1936 Yankees had five men with over one hundred runs batted in each. Name them.

1. *Max Schmeling - 1936 (by KO); Ezzard Charles - 1950 (by decision); and Rocky Marciano - 1951 (by KO).*

2. *Bill Madlock. He led the National League in hitting four times - twice with the Cubs and twice with the Pirates.*

3. *Ernie Davis of Syracuse. The Browns retired number 45 in honor of the late running back who was a victim of leukemia.*

4. *Herb Washington of the Oakland A's. He did nothing but pinch-run in his entire career.*

5. *American League: Joe DiMaggio, 56 games; National League: Pete Rose, 44 games.*

6. *Vanderbilt University, in March of 1893.*

7. *Downing: Aaron's 715th home run, in 1974; Stallard: Maris' 61st in 1961; Zachary: Ruth's 60th in 1927.*

8. *True. There was a Pittsburgh Pirates hockey team in the NHL for the 1925-1926 season. In 1930-1931, they moved to Philadelphia and became the Philadelphia Quakers. After that season, they disbanded.*

9. *Four to four. This would require that each team score exactly two safeties and nothing else.*

10. *Lou Gehrig, 152 RBI's; Joe DiMaggio, 125; Tony Lazzeri, 109; Bill Dickey, 107; George Selkirk, 107.*

1.   The Kentucky Derby is, of course, held in Kentucky. In what states are the Preakness and the Belmont Stakes held?

2.   Name five of the first six baseball Commissioners.

3.   What is the most valuable *Topps* baseball card?

4.   Before merging during the 1970 season, the AFL operated from 1960 to 1969. What player started every game for the Oakland Raiders during these ten seasons and what number did he wear?

5.   What does "no mas" mean in English? Who were the opponents in the fight associated with this phrase?

6.   In terms of innings, what is the longest game in the history of Major League baseball? What was the final score?

7.   Lew Alcindor changed his name to Kareem Abdul-Jabbar. Name the NBA teams, the college, and the high school for which he played.

8.   Six different NHL players have scored 70 or more goals in a regular season. Name at least three of them.

9.   One of the most famous homers of all time was "the shot heard 'round the world." Name the pitcher and the batter and the numbers on their uniforms.

10. The original Mets of 1962 had two pitchers with the same first and last names. Who were these pitchers?

1. The Preakness is held in Maryland; the Belmont, in New York.

2. Kenesaw Mountain Landis, Happy Chandler, Ford Frick, William Eckert, Bowie Kuhn, and Peter Ueberroth.

3. The 1952 Mickey Mantle card, which is worth more than $5,000.

4. Jim Otto, who wore number 00.

5. "No mas" means "no more." These words were spoken by Roberto Duran in the second Roberto Duran-Sugar Ray Leonard fight.

6. The Boston Braves and Brooklyn Dodgers played a 26-inning 1-1 tie, in 1920.

7. NBA: Milwaukee Bucks and Los Angeles Lakers; College: UCLA; High School: Power Memorial in New York City.

8. Wayne Gretzky, Phil Esposito, Jari Kurri, Mario Lemieux, Brett Hull, and Bernie Nicholls.

9. Bobby Thomson (number 23) hit it off Ralph Branca (number 13) during the 1951 playoff between the Dodgers and Giants.

10. Bob Miller. Robert G. Miller was a left-handed pitcher who was in his last season; Robert L. Miller was a right-handed pitcher who played for another twelve years.

1. There have been nine baseball players to win back-to-back MVP Awards. How many do you know?

2. In 1968, the horse that finished first in the Kentucky Derby was disqualified because it had run with an illegal substance in its system. Name the horse which was disqualified and the horse which was awarded first place.

3. The answer is 4,256. What's the question?

4. What Major League baseball team won the most regular season games during the 1980's?

5. What NFL player scored the most points in a season?

6. What player did Bobby Fischer defeat to win the World Chess Championship?

7. Who pitched three shutouts in one World Series?

8. What three men have coached five or more Stanley Cup winners?

9. Who is the only NBA player to win the MVP Award two consecutive years while playing for a different team each year?

10. Name the American League team and the National League team which have won the most games in a season.

1. *National League: Ernie Banks, 1958, 1959; Joe Morgan, 1975, 1976; Mike Schmidt, 1980, 1981; Dale Murphy, 1982, 1983. American League: Jimmy Foxx, 1932, 1933; Hal Newhouser, 1944, 1945; Yogi Berra, 1954, 1955; Mickey Mantle, 1956, 1957; Roger Maris, 1960, 1961.*

2. *Dancer's Image was disqualified and Forward Pass was awarded first place.*

3. *How many regular season hits did Pete Rose get?*

4. *The New York Yankees. (The Detroit Tigers were second.)*

5. *Paul Hornung of Green Bay who scored 176 points in 1960.*

6. *Boris Spassky.*

7. *Christy Mathewson, in 1905.*

8. *Toe Blake, 8 times for Montreal; Hap Day, 5 times for Toronto; Scotty Bowman, 5 times for Montreal.*

9. *Moses Malone, with Houston in 1982 and Philadelphia in 1983.*

10. *The Cleveland Indians won 111 games in 1954. (They were 111-43.) The Chicago Cubs won 116 games in 1906. (They were 116-36.)*

1. Since 1938, there have been nine different men who led their league in hitting while playing for Boston — eight for the Red Sox, one for the Braves. Name six of these men.

2. What are the nicknames of the following college football teams: Florida, Florida State, and Miami of Florida?

3. Name one of the four men to win both the Calder Trophy for Rookie of the Year and the Vezina Trophy in the same year.

4. What five baseball players have more than 3500 career hits?

5. There have been four NBA Rookies of the Year with exactly four letters in their last names. Who are they?

6. Who is the only player to win the Heisman Trophy twice?

7. Who was the first woman to compete in the Indianapolis 500?

8. In 1983, this pitcher led the Majors in wins. In 1984, he led in losses. Who is he? Hint: He won the Cy Young Award in 1983.

9. Name the only man to pitch more than one hundred games in a season.

10. Who was the Galloping Ghost and what number did he wear?

1. *Red Sox: Jimmy Foxx, Ted Williams, Billy Goodman, Pete Runnels, Carl Yastrzemski, Fred Lynn, Carney Lansford, and Wade Boggs; Braves: Ernie Lombardi.*

2. *Florida Gators, Florida State Seminoles, Miami of Florida Hurricanes.*

3. *Frank Brimsek, 1938-1939; Tony Esposito, 1969-1970; Tom Barrasso, 1983-1984; and Ed Balfour, 1990-1991.*

4. *Pete Rose, Ty Cobb, Henry Aaron, Stan Musial, and Tris Speaker.*

5. *Willis Reed, 1965; Dave Bing, 1967; Phil Ford, 1979; and Larry Bird, 1980.*

6. *Archie Griffin.*

7. *Janet Guthrie, in 1977.*

8. *LaMarr Hoyt, who had 24 wins in 1983 and 18 losses in 1984.*

9. *Mike Marshall, who pitched in 106 games in 1974.*

10. *Red Grange, 77.*

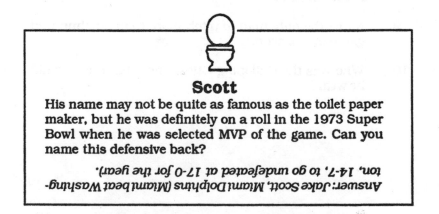

Scott

His name may not be quite as famous as the toilet paper maker, but he was definitely on a roll in the 1973 Super Bowl when he was selected MVP of the game. Can you name this defensive back?

Answer: Jake Scott, Miami Dolphins (Miami beat Washington, 14-7, to go undefeated at 17-0 for the year).

1. In 1969, the Baseball Writers' Association of America selected their All-Time Baseball Team. They picked one player for each regular position, a right-handed pitcher, a left-handed pitcher, a greatest player, and a greatest manager. How many of the all-time greats do you know?

2. What NHL player has scored the most points in a season?

3. There were three perfect games pitched during the 1960's. What three pitchers hurled them?

4. Name the two countries to win the World Cup in soccer two consecutive times.

5. Who was the first gymnast to be awarded a score of 10 in the Olympics?

6. LaMarr Hoyt is one of five Cy Young winners with exactly four letters in his last name. Do you know the others?

7. What NHL goalie once played more than 500 consecutive games?

8. Name the eight football teams in the Ivy League.

9. NBA games have been played in the following arenas. Name the cities they are located in — Cow Palace, The Kingdome, The Omni, and Cobo Hall.

10. Since 1950, what National Leaguer has had the highest batting average for a season? What American Leaguer has had the highest batting average for a season?

1. 1B - Lou Gehrig; 2B - Rogers Hornsby; SS - Honus Wagner; 3B - Pie Traynor; OF - Babe Ruth, Ty Cobb, Joe DiMaggio; C - Mickey Cochrane; RHP - Walter Johnson; LHP - Lefty Grove; Greatest Player - Babe Ruth; Greatest Manager - John McGraw.

2. Wayne Gretzky - 215.

3. Jim Bunning of the Phillies, in 1964 against the Mets; Sandy Koufax of the Dodgers, in 1965 against the Cubs; Catfish Hunter of the A's, in 1968 against the Twins.

4. Italy, in 1934 and 1938; Brazil, in 1958 and 1962.

5. Nadia Comaneci of Romania, at the 1976 Olympics, held in Montreal.

6. Early Wynn, Whitey Ford, Vida Blue, Sparky Lyle.

7. Glenn Hall of Detroit and Chicago, who played 502 consecutive games from 1955 to 1963.

8. Brown, Columbia, Cornell, Dartmouth, Harvard, Pennsylvania, Princeton, and Yale.

9. San Francisco, Seattle, Atlanta, and Detroit.

10. Tony Gwynn, who batted .370 in 1987; George Brett, who batted .390 in 1980.

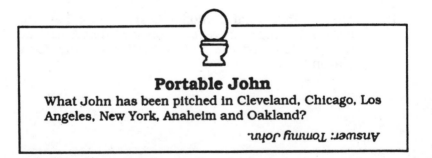

Portable John

What John has been pitched in Cleveland, Chicago, Los Angeles, New York, Anaheim and Oakland?

Answer: Tommy John.

1. In the decade of the 1970's, players from the Cincinnati Reds won the MVP Award six times. Name the four different men to do this.

2. What team did the United States hockey team defeat in 1980 to win the Olympic Gold Medal?

3. What two NFL teams merged in 1943 to become the Steagles?

4. Who holds the record for most strikeouts by a pitcher in a World Series game?

5. What harness racing driver has the most wins?

6. In 1963, two National Leaguers tied for the home run lead hitting the same number of homers as their uniform numbers. Who are these players and what number did they wear?

7. Who holds the NFL record for the highest punting average in a season?

8. What was the score of the first Super Bowl which the AFL won?

9. In the 1960's, two foreigners won the Indianapolis 500. Name them.

10. Name a Hall of Fame baseball player to have one son play Major League baseball and another son play football in the NFL.

1.   *Johnny Bench, 1970 and 1972; Pete Rose, 1973; Joe Morgan, 1975 and 1976; George Foster, 1977.*

2.   *Finland.*

3.   *The Pittsburgh Steelers and the Philadelphia Eagles.*

4.   *Bob Gibson of the Cardinals, who struck out seventeen Tigers in the opening game of the 1968 World Series.*

5.   *Herve Filion.*

6.   *Hank Aaron and Willie McCovey, 44.*

7.   *Sammy Baugh, with a 51.4 yard average.*

8.   *16 to 7, Jets over the Colts.*

9.   *Jim Clark of Scotland, in 1965; Graham Hill of England, in 1966.*

10.   *Yogi Berra. His son Dale played Major League baseball; his son Tim played NFL football.*

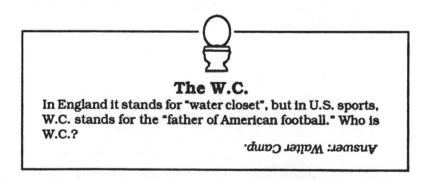

The W.C.

In England it stands for "water closet", but in U.S. sports, W.C. stands for the "father of American football." Who is W.C.?

Answer: Walter Camp.

1. The most one-sided NFL game was the 1940 Championship. What teams played and what was the final score?

2. Give the nicknames of the following college football teams — Air Force, Army, Navy.

3. Who was Joseph Barrow?

4. In 1987, Mark McGwire won the American League Rookie of the Year Award. Four other A.L. first basemen have won this Award. Name two of them.

5. The 1960 World Series was won by a ninth-inning homer over the left field fence. Name the stadium, the batter, the pitcher, the catcher, and the left fielder.

6. No horse won the Triple Crown during the 1950's and 1960's. During the 1970's, three horses won it. Which three?

7. Since 1930, four pitchers have won three games in a single World Series. Name them, the years, the teams they played for, and the teams they beat.

8. Who won the 100 meter run in the 1936 Olympics?

9. Which colleges did the following NBA stars attend — Wilt Chamberlain, Bill Russell, Moses Malone?

10. In 1971, a Pirate hit three home runs in a Divisional Playoff Game; in 1978, a Royal accomplished this feat. Can you think of these players?

1.   The Chicago Bears beat the Washington Redskins, 73-0.

2.   Air Force - Falcons; Army - Cadets; Navy - Midshipmen or Middies.

3.   Boxing's Joe Louis.

4.   Walt Dropo, 1950; Chris Chambliss, 1971; Mike Hargrove, 1974; Alvin Davis, 1984.

5.   Stadium: Forbes Field; Batter: Bill Mazeroski; Pitcher: Ralph Terry; Catcher: John Blanchard; Left Fielder: Yogi Berra.

6.   Secretariat, 1973; Seattle Slew, 1977; Affirmed, 1978.

7.   Harry Breechen, in 1946, for the St. Louis Cardinals against the Boston Red Sox; Lew Burdette, in 1957, for the Milwaukee Braves against the Yankees; Bob Gibson, in 1967, for the St. Louis Cardinals against the Red Sox; Mickey Lolich, in 1968, for the Tigers against the Cardinals.

8.   Jesse Owens.

9.   Chamberlain: Kansas; Russell: San Francisco; Malone never went to college.

10.   1971: Bob Robertson of the Pirates, against the San Francisco Giants; 1978: George Brett of the Kansas City Royals, against the Yankees.

1. Name the three men who have managed Major League baseball teams for the most years.

2. Who was the first NHL player to score more than one hundred points in a season?

3. How many men's basketball games have been lost by the United States in the Olympics?

4. What American League batting champion later became mayor of Vera Cruz, Mexico?

5. Which current NFL team did not have a winning record until its 21st year in existence?

6. In what stadiums did the Dodgers and Giants first play their home games when they moved to California for the 1958 season?

7. True or False: The NBA record for the most personal fouls in a game is eight.

8. What champion was outweighed in every one of his thirteen heavyweight title fights?

9. In the 1947 World Series, a Yankee pitcher came within one out of pitching a no-hitter. Name the pitcher and name the batter who got the hit.

10. What pro football Hall of Famer holds the college record for most points scored in a football game?

1. Connie Mack, 53 years; John McGraw, 34 years; and Bucky Harris, 29 years.

2. Phil Esposito of the Boston Bruins, who scored 126 points during the 1968-1969 season.

3. Two — both to the Soviet Union — one in 1972 and the other in 1988.

4. Bobby Avila. Avila won the 1954 batting title while playing for the Cleveland Indians.

5. New Orleans Saints.

6. Dodgers - Los Angeles Coliseum; Giants - Seal Stadium.

7. True. In a 1949 game, Don Otten of Tri-Cities committed eight personal fouls.

8. Floyd Patterson.

9. Bill Bevens was pitching the no-hitter but had given up ten walks. Cookie Lavagetto pinch-hit for the Dodgers and hit a double off the right field wall to knock home two runs and win the game for the Dodgers, 2 to 1.

10. Jimmy Brown of Syracuse, who scored 43 points in a 1956 game.

1. There have been four World Series games which have been won 1-0 with the one run being scored on a home run. It happened once in 1923, once in 1949, and twice in 1966. Who were the four men to hit the home runs?

2. In 1976, Muhammad Ali fought a wrestler in an exhibition. Who was this Japanese wrestler?

3. From the 1957-1958 season to the 1973-1974 season, only three men led the NBA in rebounds. Who were they?

4. The 1956 Cincinnati Reds hit 221 home runs to set the National League record for most home runs hit by a team. Eight players hit ten or more homers. How many can you name?

5. Indianapolis, Anderson, Tri-Cities, Sheboygan, Waterloo, and Denver comprised the Western Division of what professional major league sport?

6. One brother led the American League in hitting, the other gained over one thousand yards in an NFL season. Who are these brothers?

7. What Notre Dame player was an NBA Number 1 Draft pick?

8. Who was the first President of the United States to attend a Monday Night Football Game?

9. What athlete has played Major League baseball, played NBA basketball, and has won a gold medal in the Olympics?

10. Since 1970, two pitchers have both won and lost twenty games in the same season. Who are they?

1.   1923: *Casey Stengel of the New York Giants, against the Yankees; 1949: Tommy Henrich of the New York Yankees, against the Dodgers; 1966: Paul Blair and Frank Robinson of the Baltimore Orioles, against the Dodgers. Note: Henrich hit his leading off the bottom of the ninth to win the game.*

2.   *Antonio Inoki.*

3.   *Bill Russell, Wilt Chamberlain, and Elvin Hayes.*

4.   *Frank Robinson, 38; Wally Post, 36; Ted Kluszewski, 35; Gus Bell, 29; Ed Bailey, 28; Ray Jablonski, 15; Smokey Burgess, 12; George Crowe, 10.*

5.   *The 1949-1950 NBA.*

6.   *The Johnsons. Alex Johnson, while playing for California, won the American League batting title in 1970. Brother Ron twice rushed for over one thousand yards with the New York Giants.*

7.   *Austin Carr, who was picked by Cleveland in 1971.*

8.   *Jimmy Carter, in 1978. He saw the Washington Redskins defeat the Dallas Cowboys, 9 to 5.*

9.   *Gene Conley.*

10.   *Phil Niekro, in 1979, when he was 21-20 with the Braves; Wilbur Wood, in 1973, when he was 24-20 with the White Sox.*

1.   Who is the youngest man to be an NBA coach?

2.   Only two men managed teams to American League pennants during the 1950's. Who are they?

3.   Who has scored the most points in an NHL game?

4.   Who played in the Majors, had a son who played in the Majors, and was an umpire in the Majors?

5.   What four American women have won Olympic golds for figure skating in Women's Singles?

6.   Tim Brown won the Heisman Trophy in 1987. Name the other six Notre Dame Heisman winners.

7.   Five men have managed pennant-winning teams in each league. Who?

8.   Who was the first pitcher to win a World Series game for a National League expansion team? Who did it for an American League expansion team?

9.   How many players play for a rugby team, a soccer team, a cricket team, and a men's lacrosse team?

10.   Who is the only Brave to play for Boston, Milwaukee, and Atlanta?

1. *Dave DeBusschere, who was named coach of the Detroit Pistons at 24.*

2. *Al Lopez and Casey Stengel. Lopez won in 1954 with the Cleveland Indians and in 1959 with the Chicago White Sox; Stengel won the other eight years with the Yankees.*

3. *Darryl Sittler of the Toronto Maple Leafs, who scored ten points in a game against the Boston Bruins in 1976.*

4. *Bill Kunkel.*

5. *Tenley Albright, 1956; Carol Heiss, 1960; Peggy Fleming, 1968; Dorothy Hamill, 1976.*

6. *Angelo Bertelli, 1943; Johnny Lujack, 1947; Leon Hart, 1949; John Lattner, 1953; Paul Hornung, 1956; and John Huarte, 1964.*

7. *Joe McCarthy, Cubs and Yankees; Yogi Berra, Yankees and Mets; Al Dark, Giants and A's; Sparky Anderson, Reds and Tigers; Dick Williams, Red Sox, A's and Padres. Anderson is the only man to have won a World Series in each league.*

8. *National League: Jerry Koosman of the 1969 Mets, against the Baltimore Orioles; American League: Dan Quisenberry of the Kansas City Royals, in 1980, against the Phillies.*

9. *Rugby, 15; soccer, 11; cricket, 11; men's lacrosse, 10.*

10. *Ed Mathews.*

1. Name three men who knocked down Joe Louis when he was heavyweight champion of the world.

2. In auto racing, what do the following flags indicate: green, red, white, and checkered?

3. What U.S. Senator is a member of the Basketball Hall of Fame?

4. What father and son played on the gold medal-winning United States Olympic hockey teams in 1960 and 1980, respectively?

5. How many Boston Celtics have led the NBA in scoring?

6. Who is Arnold Raymond Cream?

7. What football Hall of Famer also played in a World Series game?

8. Name the first Olympian to play pro football.

9. Four sportswriters have won Pulitzer Prizes. Give two of them.

10. What Tiger holds the Major League record for most home runs in a month?

1. Tony Galento and Buddy Baer each did it once; Jersey Joe Walcott knocked him down three times.

2. Green - start of the race; red - stop because of unsafe conditions; white - beginning the last lap; and checkered - end of the race.

3. Bill Bradley of New Jersey, who played his college ball at Princeton.

4. Father: Bill Christian; Son: Dave Christian.

5. None.

6. Jersey Joe Walcott.

7. Jim Thorpe, in the 1917 World Series for the Giants.

8. Jim Thorpe.

9. Arthur Daley, Red Smith, and Dave Anderson of The New York Times and Jim Murray of The Los Angeles Times.

10. Rudy York - 18.

1. Name the eight original AFL teams.

2. Summer Olympics have been held in the United States three times. In which cities and in what years?

3. With what four teams did Roger Maris play in his twelve-year career?

4. What NBA basketball team went 40-1 at home one season?

5. What six National League Rookies of the Year have exactly four letters in their last names?

6. Name one of two men to play on an NCAA title-winning basketball team and to coach one.

7. When he was inducted into the Baseball Hall of Fame in 1989, this player became the first Little Leaguer ever awarded that honor. Do you know him?

8. In 1983, the United States lost the America's Cup for the first time since 1851. Name the winning and losing boats.

9. What are the first and middle names of the three DiMaggio brothers?

10. Name the three San Diego pitchers who have won the Cy Young Award.

1. *Boston Patriots, Buffalo Bills, Dallas Texans, Denver Broncos, Houston Oilers, Los Angeles Chargers, New York Titans, Oakland Raiders.*

2. *St. Louis, in 1904; Los Angeles, in 1932 and 1984. Atlanta will host the games in 1996.*

3. *Cleveland Indians, Kansas City A's, New York Yankees, and St. Louis Cardinals.*

4. *The 1985 - '86 Boston Celtics.*

5. *Alvin Dark, 1948; Willie Mays, 1951; Wally Moon, 1954; Pete Rose, 1963; Steve Howe, 1980; and Chris Sabo, 1988.*

6. *Dean Smith, who played at Kansas and coached North Carolina, and Bobby Knight, who played at Ohio State and coached Indiana.*

7. *Carl Yastrzemski.*

8. *Australia II defeated Liberty.*

9. *Dominic Paul, Joseph Paul, and Vincent Paul.*

10. *Randy Jones, 1976; Gaylord Perry, 1978; and Mark Davis, 1989.*

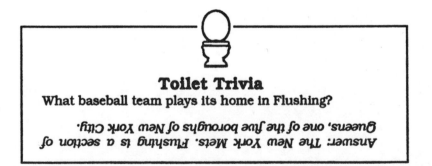

Toilet Trivia
What baseball team plays its home in Flushing?

Answer: The New York Mets. Flushing is a section of Queens, one of the five boroughs of New York City.

1. Super Bowl XXII was played in San Diego's Jack Murphy Stadium, in 1988. In baseball, it was also the site of the Padres home games for the 1984 Fall Classic, making it only the second stadium to host a World Series and a Super Bowl. Do you know the other?

2. What NHL player won eight straight MVP Awards?

3. What NFL team holds the record for the most consecutive losses?

4. What right-handed batter has the most American League home runs? What left-handed batter? What switch-hitter? What right-handed batter has the most National League home runs? What left-handed batter? What switch-hitter?

5. Who is the only NBA player to have led the league in scoring, assists and rebounds at various times in his career?

6. Name the left-handed and right-handed pitchers with the most career Major League wins.

7. What is the record for the most runs scored in an inning — 14, 17, or 20?

8. Three horses with the initials "S.S." have won the Preakness. Give two of them.

9. What was the year and site of the first Olympic Games not held in Europe or North America?

10. There have been six baseball Rookies of the Year who have won the award playing for Boston. How many do you know?

1. *The Los Angeles Memorial Coliseum, where the first Super Bowl was played in 1967 and where the Dodgers played their home games in the 1959 World Series. (Dodger Stadium was not built until 1962.)*

2. *Wayne Gretzky, who won it from 1980 to 1987.*

3. *The Tampa Bay Buccaneers, 26, in 1976 and 1977.*

4. *American League: right-handed - Harmon Killebrew, 573; left-handed - Babe Ruth, 708; switch-hitter - Mickey Mantle, 536. National League: right-handed - Hank Aaron, 733; left-handed - Willie McCovey, 521; switch-hitter - Ted Simmons, 182.*

5. *Wilt Chamberlain.*

6. *Left-handed: Warren Spahn, 363. Right-handed: Cy Young, 511.*

7. *17, which the Red Sox got against the St. Louis Browns, in 1953.*

8. *Seattle Slew - 1977; Sunday Silence - 1989; and Summer Squall - 1990.*

9. *1956, in Melbourne, Australia.*

10. *Braves: Alvin Dark, 1948; Sam Jethroe, 1950. Red Sox: Walt Dropo, 1950; Don Schwall, 1961; Carlton Fisk, 1952; Fred Lynn, 1975.*

1. Who are the four men to have pitched more than 900 games in the Majors?

2. Paul Newman has starred in a boxing movie, a hockey movie, two movies about pool, and a movie about auto racing. How many of these five can you get?

3. In the 1980's, four women won the Singles Championship at Wimbledon. Name them all.

4. Who is the only man to lead both Major Leagues in steals?

5. With his victory over Larry Holmes, Michael Spinks became the sixth heavyweight champion to have won a gold medal in the Olympics. Who are the others?

6. In 1963, two future Hall of Fame pitchers were locked in a sixteen-inning scoreless duel until Willie Mays hit a homer to win the game, 1-0. Who were the pitchers?

7. What university won nine consecutive wrestling titles, from 1978 to 1986?

8. True or False: Wilt Chamberlain was a head coach in the ABA.

9. Name one of the two members of Fordham's Seven Blocks of Granite who are in the Pro Football Hall of Fame.

10. San Francisco and Cincinnati have met in the Super Bowl twice. Name the starting quarterbacks.

1. *Hoyt Wilhelm, Lindy McDaniel, Cy Young, and Rollie Fingers.*

2. *Boxing:* Somebody Up There Likes Me, *the biography of Rocky Graziano; Hockey:* Slapshot; *Pool:* The Hustler *and* The Color of Money; *and Auto Racing:* Winning.

3. *Evonne Goolagong Cawley - 1980; Chris Evert Lloyd - 1981; Martina Navratilova - 1982 through 1987; and Steffi Graf - 1988 and 1989.*

4. *Ron LeFlore, who did it with Montreal and Detroit.*

5. *Floyd Patterson, Muhammad Ali, Joe Frazier, George Foreman, and Leon Spinks.*

6. *Juan Marichal and Warren Spahn.*

7. *Iowa.*

8. *True. He coached the San Diego Conquistadors to a 37-47 record in 1973-1974.*

9. *Vince Lombardi and Alex Wojciechowicz.*

10. *San Francisco: Joe Montana each time; Cincinnati: Kenny Anderson and Boomer Esiason.*

1. Name the West German- born player who ended Bjorn Borg's string of consecutive Wimbledon titles at five in 1981.

2. Prior to Michael Jordan, there had been five NBA players who had led the league in scoring for at least three consecutive years. Who are they?

3. Name the first three NHL players to score fifty goals in a regular season.

4. Where are the following Halls of Fame located — baseball, pro football, basketball, pro hockey?

5. How many regular season lifetime home runs did Hank Aaron hit? How many did Babe Ruth hit?

6. Who is the only boxer to fight both Muhammad Ali and Rocky Marciano?

7. The only British runner ever to win a gold medal in the 100 meter run in the Olympics accomplished the task in the 1924 Olympics. He was portrayed by Ben Cross in an Oscar-winning film. Can you come up with the name of the runner and the movie?

8. There are five Division I football teams beginning with the letter "H". Name them.

9. What two players did the Yankees honor when they retired uniform number 8? Hint: They were both catchers.

10. What is a more appropriate name for an eagle on a par three golf hole?

1.   *John McEnroe.*

2.   *George Mikan, 1949-1951; Neil Johnston, 1953-1955; Wilt Chamberlain, 1960-1966; Bob McAdoo, 1974-1976; George Gervin, 1978-1980.*

3.   *Maurice Richard, 1946-1947; Bernie "Boom-Boom" Geoffrion, 1960-1961; Bobby Hull, 1961-1962.*

4.   *Baseball - Cooperstown, New York; pro football - Canton, Ohio; basketball - Springfield, Massachusetts; pro hockey - Toronto, Ontario.*

5.   *Aaron - 755; Ruth - 714.*

6.   *Archie Moore, who fought against Muhammad Ali (when he was still known as Cassius Clay) in 1962 and against Rocky Marciano in 1955, losing both times.*

7.   *Harold Abrahams. The movie was* Chariots of Fire.

8.   *Harvard, Hawaii, Holy Cross, Houston, Howard.*

9.   *Bill Dickey and Yogi Berra.*

10.   *A hole-in-one.*

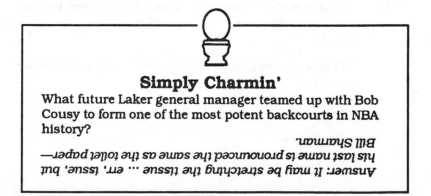

Simply Charmin'

What future Laker general manager teamed up with Bob Cousy to form one of the most potent backcourts in NBA history?

Answer: It may be stretching the tissue ... err, tissue, but his last name is pronounced the same as the toilet paper— Bill Sharman.

1. What father and two sons played for the same NHL team at the same time?

2. How many times did Wilt Chamberlain foul out of an NBA game?

3. What Hall of Famer was on the cover of the first issue of *Sports Illustrated*?

4. What are the nicknames of the following three Hall of Fame pitchers: Christy Mathewson, Mordecai Brown, Walter Johnson?

5. The movie *Raging Bull* was about what boxer? Who portrayed him?

6. True or False: A player has hit home runs in his first two times up in the Majors.

7. In 1978, Affirmed won the Triple Crown. What horse finished second to him in all three races?

8. Who is the only player to quarterback a team in a Rose Bowl, a Grey Cup, and a Super Bowl?

9. What American League right-handed batter has hit the most home runs in a season? What left-handed batter? What switch-hitter? What National league right-handed batter has hit the most home runs in a season? What left-handed batter? What switch-hitter?

10. Who was the winning pitcher in the 1988 Olympic Gold Medal baseball game?

1.   *Gordie Howe and his sons, Mark and Marty, played in the NHL for the Hartford Whalers.*

2.   *None.*

3.   *Eddie Mathews.*

4.   *Mathewson: Big Six; Brown: Three Finger; Johnson: Big Train.*

5.   *Jake LaMotta, portrayed by Robert DeNiro in an Oscar-winning performance.*

6.   *True. Bob Nieman of the St. Louis Browns did this in 1951.*

7.   *Alydar.*

8.   *Joe Kapp. He quarterbacked California in the Rose Bowl, British Columbia in the Grey Cup, and Minnesota in the Super Bowl.*

9.   *American League: right-handed - Hank Greenberg and Jimmie Foxx, 58; left-handed - Roger Maris, 61; switch-hitter - Mickey Mantle, 54; National League: right-handed - Hack Wilson, 56; left-handed - John Mize, 51; switch-hitter - Howard Johnson, 36.*

10.   *Jim Abbott.*

1.   What player who won a Major Amateur Golf Championship has a father who won an Oscar for Best Actor?

2.   Give the Division I college football teams which have the following nicknames — the Crimson Tide, the Red Raiders and the Crimson.

3.   What Major Leaguer has led off the game with a home run the most times?

4.   From 1962 to 1966, the Cy Young winner pitched for Los Angeles. Name these three men.

5.   In the 1970's, the AFC won eight Super Bowls. What NFC team won the other two?

6.   Name the first NBA player to score 20,000 career regular season points. Who was the first to score 30,000 points?

7.   The 1973 Atlanta Braves had three players who hit forty or more home runs. Who were they?

8.   Who pitched the most Major League games?

9.   Name the man who coached a Super Bowl team and played in the NBA.

10. Who am I? I have been an All-Star catcher many times and my father led the American League in RBI's in 1955.

1.   *Nathaniel Crosby, who won the United States Ama-*
      teur Championship in 1981.

2.   *Crimson Tide: Alabama; Red Raiders: Colgate or*
      Texas Tech; Crimson: Harvard.

3.   *Rickey Henderson.*

4.   *Sandy Koufax of the Los Angeles Dodgers in 1963,*
      1965, and 1966; Don Drysdale of the Dodgers in
      1962; Dean Chance of the Los Angeles Angels in
      1964. Note: the Los Angeles Angels changed their
      name to the California Angels in 1965.

5.   *The Dallas Cowboys.*

6.   *20,000: Bob Pettit; 30,000: Wilt Chamberlain.*

7.   *Davey Johnson, 43; Darrell Evans, 41; Hank Aaron,*
      40.

8.   *Hoyt Wilhelm, 1070 games.*

9.   *Bud Grant, who coached the NFL Vikings and played*
      for the 1950-1951 Minneapolis Lakers.

10.   *Bob Boone. His father, Ray, led the league while with*
      Detroit.

1. Name the winning quarterback in each of the first four Super Bowls.

2. There have been five American League Rookies of the Year having exactly four letters in their last names. How many can you name?

3. Whose beating at the hands of Larry Holmes in 1982 prompted Howard Cosell to decide to stop announcing boxing?

4. What future Hall of Famer gave up Willie Mays' first home run, in 1951?

5. Who is the youngest man ever to win a Grand Slam tennis event?

6. What Raider played in Super Bowls in three decades?

7. In addition to winning singles titles, John McEnroe and Martina Navratilova have won doubles titles at the U.S. Open. Who were their partners?

8. Jim Thorpe was a member of what Indian tribe?

9. Who's the only man other than Bo Jackson to win the Heisman Trophy and play Major League baseball?

10. There are two pairs of brothers who pitched in the Majors with each hurler winning over two hundred games. Who are they?

1. *I and II: Bart Starr of Green Bay; III: Joe Namath of the New York Jets; IV: Len Dawson of Kansas City.*

2. *Harry Byrd, 1952; Bob Grim, 1954; Tommy Agee, 1966; Carlton Fisk, 1972; Fred Lynn, 1975.*

3. *Tex Cobb.*

4. *Warren Spahn.*

5. *Michael Chang, who was 17 when he won the French Open in 1989.*

6. *Gene Upshaw, in 1968, 1977, and 1981.*

7. *McEnroe: Peter Fleming and Mark Woodforde; Navratilova: Betty Stove, Billie Jean King, Pam Shriver, Hana Mandlikova, and Gigi Fernandez.*

8. *Sac and Fox.*

9. *Vic Janowicz. He won the Heisman in 1950 while playing for Ohio State. In 1953 and 1954, he played baseball for the Pittsburgh Pirates, batting only .214 in 83 games.*

10. *Gaylord and Jim Perry and Phil and Joe Niekro.*

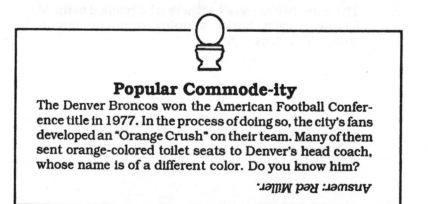

Popular Commode-ity

The Denver Broncos won the American Football Conference title in 1977. In the process of doing so, the city's fans developed an "Orange Crush" on their team. Many of them sent orange-colored toilet seats to Denver's head coach, whose name is of a different color. Do you know him?

Answer: Red Miller.

1. Four ABA teams joined the NBA in 1977. Name them.

2. Who is the only baseball player to have been named Most Valuable Player in both leagues?

3. Who's the only person to have played Wimbledon and to have had a major role in a James Bond movie?

4. It has happened three times in the history of baseball that two men have hit fifty or more home runs in the same season. Can you name the years and players?

5. Name the two boxers who knocked out Joe Louis.

6. Walter Johnson threw more than 3,000 strikeouts while playing for just one club (the Washington Senators) his entire career. Only one other pitcher can make that claim. Who is he?

7. Who was the smallest Major Leaguer and what number did he wear?

8. Which professional football team was the first to put emblems on their helmets?

9. Who is the only player to lead the Majors in home runs and E.R.A.?

10. Ronald Reagan is known for portraying a famous baseball player and a famous football player. Can you name them?

1. *Denver Nuggets, Indiana Pacers, New Jersey Nets, and San Antonio Spurs.*

2. *Frank Robinson (in 1961, with the Cincinnati Reds and, in 1966, with the Baltimore Orioles).*

3. *Vijay Amritraj, who played Wimbledon both before and after his role in* Octopussy.

4. *1938: Hank Greenberg, 58, and Jimmie Foxx, 50; 1947: Ralph Kiner, 51, and Johnny Mize, 51; 1961: Roger Maris, 61, and Mickey Mantle, 54.*

5. *Max Schmeling and Rocky Marciano.*

6. *Bob Gibson of the St. Louis Cardinals, with 3117.*

7. *Eddie Gaedel of the St. Louis Browns, who was 3 feet 7 inches tall and weighed 65 pounds. His number was 1/8.*

8. *The Los Angeles Rams of 1948.*

9. *Babe Ruth.*

10. *Baseball: Grover Cleveland Alexander; Football: George Gipp.*

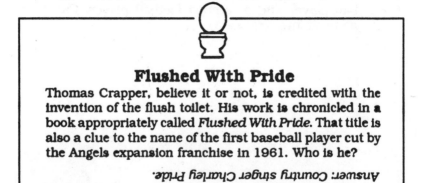

Flushed With Pride

Thomas Crapper, believe it or not, is credited with the invention of the flush toilet. His work is chronicled in a book appropriately called *Flushed With Pride*. That title is also a clue to the name of the first baseball player cut by the Angels expansion franchise in 1961. Who is he?

Answer: Country singer Charley Pride.

1. Four men coached the same NFL teams for over twenty consecutive years. Who are they? Can you name the four teams?

2. Who was the only man in the last fifty years to lose three games in the same World Series?

3. What heavyweight fighter won the gold medal three times in the Olympics?

4. Who was the first Hispanic to win the American League MVP Award? And the first Hispanic to win the National League MVP Award?

5. True or False: It is legal in the NFL to punt the ball when you are passed the line of scrimmage.

6. Who is the only pitcher to win more than 200 games in each Major League?

7. Who is the youngest winner of the Men's Singles Title at Wimbledon?

8. For a while in the 1960's, the Dodgers had a starting infield of all switch-hitters. Name these four players.

9. For what teams did Bill Russell and Bob Cousy play their last NBA games?

10. Who is the only man to win the Cy Young Award while pitching for two teams in the same season?

1. Curly Lambeau of Green Bay, Tom Landry of Dallas, Steve Owen of the New York Giants, and Don Shula of the Miami Dolphins.

2. George Frazier of the New York Yankees, in 1981.

3. Teofilo Stevenson of Cuba, in 1972, 1976, and 1980.

4. American League: Zoilo Versailles, Cuban, 1965. National League: Roberto Clemente, Puerto Rican, 1966.

5. True.

6. Cy Young.

7. Boris Becker of Germany, who was 17 when he won the title in 1985.

8. Wes Parker, Jim Lefebvre, Jim Gilliam, and Maury Wills.

9. Russell: Boston Celtics; Cousy: Cincinnati Royals.

10. Rick Sutcliffe. In fact, he pitched for two different leagues when he did it in 1984. He started the year with the Cleveland Indians and had a record of 4-5 with them; he then went to the Cubs and was 16-1 for Chicago.

1. Give the top five home run hitters of all time and the team with which each player ended his career.

2. Who was the first high school runner to officially break the four minute mile?

3. Although it hadn't happened since the 1920's, two horses with three words in their names won the Kentucky Derby in the 1980's. Name one of them.

4. Who pitched two consecutive no-hitters?

5. Who was the first golfer to shoot a score lower than his age in a round of a PGA tournament?

6. Who comprised the Los Angeles Rams "Fearsome Foursome"?

7. Who holds the American League record for most consecutive games played? Who holds the National League record?

8. What Washington Redskin defensive back led the league in interceptions in 1943?

9. Who is credited with inventing basketball?

10. Name the two Major League pitchers with exactly 300 wins.

Answers

1. *Hank Aaron, Milwaukee Brewers; Babe Ruth, Boston Braves; Willie Mays, New York Mets; Frank Robinson, Cleveland Indians; Harmon Killebrew, Kansas City Royals.*

2. *Jim Ryun.*

3. *Gato del Sol, in 1982; Spend a Buck, in 1985.*

4. *Johnny Vander Meer of the Cincinnati Reds.*

5. *Sam Snead. In 1979, at the age of 67, he shot a 66 at the Quad Cities Open.*

6. *Rosey Grier, Deacon Jones, Lamar Lundy, and Merlin Olsen.*

7. *Lou Gehrig, with 2130 consecutive games, holds the American League record. Steve Garvey holds the NL record with 1207.*

8. *Sammy Baugh, 11.*

9. *Dr. James Naismith.*

10. *Early Wynn and Lefty Grove.*

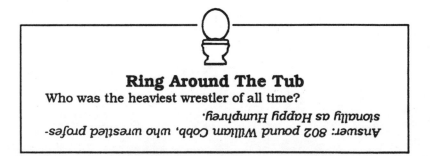

Ring Around The Tub
Who was the heaviest wrestler of all time?

Answer: 802 pound William Cobb, who wrestled professionally as Happy Humphrey.

1.   Name the two teams that played in the last American Football League Championship Game. Who won?

2.   In 1965, a National League pitcher hurled nine innings of no-hit ball and found himself locked in a scoreless duel at the end of nine. In fact, this happened to him twice that season. Who is this pitcher?

3.   Who is the oldest jockey to win the Kentucky Derby?

4.   The Little Brown Jug is the oldest football trophy. It is awarded annually to the winner of what college football game?

5.   What are the ten events of the decathlon?

6.   What American League batter led his league in hitting for the most consecutive years? For how many years? What National League batter led his league for the most consecutive years? How many years?

7.   Who was the first golfer to win all four professional Majors: the British and U.S. Opens, the Masters, and the PGA?

8.   What do quarterback Y.A. Tittle's initials stand for?

9.   UCLA won the NCAA Basketball Championship nine times in the ten-year period 1964-1973. Which college won it the other time?

10.   Two Major Leaguers have hit home runs as teenagers and when they were over forty. Name one of them.

1. *The Kansas City Chiefs beat the Oakland Raiders, 17-7. The Chiefs then went on to defeat the Minnesota Vikings in the last AFL-NFL Super Bowl, 23-7.*

2. *Jim Maloney of the Reds. He lost one game, 1-0, to the Mets giving up a home run to Johnny Lewis in extra innings and he beat the Cubs, 1-0, with a no-hitter.*

3. *Willie Shoemaker, who was 54 when he won on Ferdinand in 1986.*

4. *Michigan — Minnesota.*

5. *100 meter run, 400 meter run, 1500 meter run, long jump, high jump, 110 meter hurdles, shot put, javelin throw, discus throw, pole vault.*

6. *American League: Ty Cobb - nine (1907-1915); National League: Rogers Hornsby - six (1920-1925).*

7. *Gene Sarazen. He won the U.S. Open and the PGA in 1922, the British Open in 1932, and the Masters in 1935.*

8. *Yelberton Abraham.*

9. *Texas Western, in 1966. Texas Western is now known as Texas El Paso.*

10. *Ty Cobb and Rusty Staub.*

1. Name two brothers who fought for the heavyweight championship during the first half of this century. Note: They did not fight against each other.

2. Who's the last American Leaguer to win the Triple Crown? How about the last National Leaguer?

3. A member of the Baseball Hall of Fame got up exactly once in the Majors and struck out. Who?

4. Elgin Baylor and Jerry West were two stars of the Los Angeles Lakers. What colleges did they attend?

5. Who was the first black American League MVP? Who was the first black National League MVP?

6. From its inaugural in 1900 until 1975, only four countries won the Davis Cup. Name all four.

7. Who pitched 12 innings of perfect ball only to see the leadoff batter in the thirteenth reach base on an error? Who made the error? Who got the first hit of the game?

8. There are ten Canadian Football League teams. How many can you name?

9. Of all the players whose last names begin with "Q", who has hit the most homers?

10. Who's the first man to hit a golf ball which did not land on this planet?

1.   *Max and Buddy Baer.*

2.   *American League: Carl Yastrzemski, in 1967; National League: Joe Medwick, in 1937.*

3.   *Walt Alston, who played for the St. Louis Cardinals.*

4.   *Baylor: Seattle; West: West Virginia.*

5.   *American League: Elston Howard, in 1963; National League: Jackie Robinson, in 1949. By the time the AL had its first, the NL already had eleven.*

6.   *The United States, England, France, and Australia.*

7.   *Harvey Haddix of the Pittsburgh Pirates. In the thirteenth inning, Don Hoak, the third baseman, made an error to allow a man to reach first. After a sacrifice, Hank Aaron was intentionally walked. Joe Adcock of the Braves then hit a shot over the fence for an apparent home run. However, he passed Aaron on the bases between first and second and was given credit for a single. Since that was the second out of the inning, the man on second was allowed to score to make Haddix a 1-0 loser.*

8.   *British Columbia Lions, Calgary Stampeders, Edmonton Eskimos, Hamilton Tiger-Cats, Montreal Concordes, Ottawa Rough Riders, Saskatchewan Roughriders, Toronto Argonauts, and Winnipeg Blue Bombers.*

9.   *Jamie Quirk.*

10.   *Astronaut Alan B. Shepard, who hit a golf shot on the moon, in 1971.*

1. What NHL goalie has the record for the most career shutouts?

2. Who was the last Washington Senator to lead his league in home runs?

3. One NFL team went undefeated in a season. What team and what year?

4. Three pitchers have won a World Series game in the year in which they won Rookie of the Year. Name these pitchers.

5. In the first eighty years of this century, there were four heavyweight boxing champions who were not citizens of the United States. Who were they?

6. Of all the players who have ever played Major League baseball, who comes first alphabetically? Who comes second? What pitcher comes first?

7. Mark Spitz won seven gold medals in the 1972 Olympics — four for individual events, three for relays. How many of them can you name?

8. Three times in World Series history a player has hit three home runs in a game. Name the players to do this.

9. What is the maximum number of clubs you are allowed to carry in a golf match.

10. When the NFL and AFL merged, three NFL teams moved into the AFC. Which teams were they?

1. *Terry Sawchuk, with 103.*

2. *Frank Howard, in 1970.*

3. *The 1972 Miami Dolphins went 14-0 in the regular season and 3-0 in the playoffs.*

4. *Joe Black in 1952, Pat Zachry in 1976, and Fernando Valenzuela in 1981. They all won their World Series games against the Yankees.*

5. *Tommy Burns (Canada) held the crown from 1906-08; Max Schmeling (Germany), 1930-32; Primo Carnera (Italy), 1933-34; Ingemar Johansson (Sweden), 1959-60.*

6. *Hank Aaron; Tommie Aaron; Don Aase.*

7. *Individual: 100 meter butterfly, 200 meter butterfly, 100 meter freestyle, 200 meter freestyle. Relays: 400 meter freestyle, 800 meter freestyle, 400 meter medley.*

8. *Babe Ruth, in 1926 and 1928; Reggie Jackson, in 1977.*

9. *Fourteen.*

10. *Baltimore Colts, Pittsburgh Steelers, Cleveland Browns.*

1. Name the first three black managers in Major League baseball. Can you name the teams which they managed?

2. Who was the first Heisman Trophy winner?

3. What female tennis player has won the most consecutive matches, 74? For extra credit, can you name the player who stopped her streak?

4. In the last fifty years, only one Major League team had an outfield in which all three players had over 100 runs batted in. The team was the 1984 Red Sox. Can you name the three players?

5. Who was the winner of the first Women's Marathon held in the Olympics?

6. The 1968 World Champion Detroit Tigers had two future Hall of Famers playing for them. Who were they?

7. What team won the first American Football League Championship?

8. Who kicked the longest field goal in NFL history and how long was it?

9. Who was the youngest person ever to play Major League baseball? And the oldest?

10. Of all the golfers to ever win a Major, alphabetically who is last?

1. *Frank Robinson - Cleveland Indians, 1975; Larry Doby - Chicago White Sox, 1978; Maury Wills - Seattle Mariners, 1980.*

2. *Jay Berwanger of the University of Chicago, in 1935.*

3. *Martina Navratilova. Helena Sukova beat her to end the streak.*

4. *Tony Armas, Dwight Evans, and Jim Rice.*

5. *Joan Benoit, in 1984.*

6. *Al Kaline and Eddie Mathews.*

7. *In the 1960 AFL Championship Game, the Houston Oilers beat the Los Angeles Chargers, 24-16.*

8. *Tom Dempsey of the New Orleans Saints - 63 yards.*

9. *Joe Nuxhall, who pitched when he was 15 years old for the Cincinnati Reds during the war year of 1944. Satchel Paige was 59 when he hurled in a game for the Kansas City A's in 1965.*

10. *Fuzzy Zoeller.*

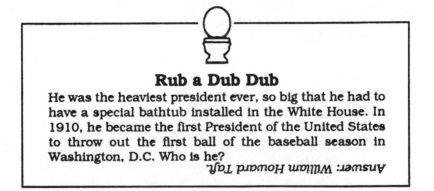

Rub a Dub Dub

He was the heaviest president ever, so big that he had to have a special bathtub installed in the White House. In 1910, he became the first President of the United States to throw out the first ball of the baseball season in Washington, D.C. Who is he?

Answer: William Howard Taft.

The Bathroom Library

THE BATHROOM BASKETBALL BOOK
THE BATHROOM GUEST BOOK
THE BATHROOM CROSSWORD PUZZLE BOOK
THE BATHROOM DIGEST
THE BATHROOM TRIVIA BOOK
THE BATHROOM ENTERTAINMENT BOOK
THE BATHROOM SPORTS QUIZ BOOK
THE BATHROOM SPORTS QUOTE BOOK
THE BATHROOM GAME BOOK
THE BATHROOM BASEBALL BOOK
THE BATHROOM FOOTBALL BOOK
THE BATHROOM GOLF BOOK
THE BATHROOM SOAP OPERA BOOK
THE BATHROOM INSPIRATION BOOK

For further information, write to:
Red-Letter Press, Inc.
P.O. Box 393,
Saddle River, N.J. 07458